Circular Communities

Els Leclercq
Mo Smit

nai010 publishers

Contents

Foreword	5
Introduction	7
Why This Book?	8
The Transition to a Circular Economy	10
Citizens in Action in Their Own Neighbourhood	14
The New Environment and Planning Act	17
The Selected Cases	19
Reader's Guide	21
The Circular Value Flower	25
Layers of the Circular Value Flower	28
The Value Flower Field Map	32
Choices Made	34
Practical Examples	37
Afrikaanderwijk Coöperatie, Afrikaanderwijk, Rotterdam	38
I'M Binck, The Binckhorst, The Hague	54
Schoonschip, Buiksloterham, Amsterdam	70
DeBlauweWij(k)Economie, Spijkerkwartier, Arnhem	84
Plant je Vlag - IEWAN, De Vossenpels, Nijmegen	98
Delfshaven Coöperatie, Bospolder Tussendijken (BoTu), Rotterdam	112
Heliport Groen Initiatief, Heliport, Rotterdam	126
Insights Gained	141
Towards a Truly Changed Playing Field	143
Resource Cycles, Spatial Interventions and Value Creation	148
From Analysis Method to Design Method	149
Lessons	150
Bibliography and Resources	154
Image Credits	158
About the Authors	159
Credits	160

Foreword

If you ask a person what a circular neighbourhood means, chances are the answer will be *a green neighbourhood*. The idea that a circular economy is about using resources as efficiently as possible – the shortest definition I have ever heard – is a tricky concept for many people.

In 2021, our organization Milieu Centraal was asked to carry out an exploration of circular neighbourhoods. How do people see a circular neighbourhood and what can the central government do to encourage the development of these neighbourhoods? Not surprisingly, the exploration concluded that 'practise what you preach', in short, setting a good example, should be the role of central government and additionally that local councils have a crucial role to play in stimulating and scaling up circular initiatives at neighbourhood level.

The crux of the matter is often this: the local council can turn out to be a difficult partner for residents of a neighbourhood, city or village. There is not always sympathy for local initiatives, and even if there is, it is difficult to navigate across various departments to free up budget, knowledge and expertise for citizens' initiatives. And of course there are plenty of other transitions that need attention. Real systemic change, another concept that is difficult to grasp, requires time, energy, goodwill and commitment from a great many parties.

A good starting point is to set a speck on the horizon with all the preferably sympathetic parties that are involved, to ask the question: what form should the circular neighbourhood take? You then work towards that goal together, step by step. With all the parties, you formulate answers to these questions: 'What kind of neighbourhood do I want to live in, what is our dream for the neighbourhood and who are all the participants here?' New, local forms of organization with a large (or larger) role for citizens and businesses, together with local authorities, will be indispensable in this respect. Collaborating at the neighbourhood level is powerful, with people pursuing the same goal: creating a pleasant living environment. Discovering shared values, requirements and dreams makes it easier to implement changes.

To realize systemic change, sharing lessons, resources and skills is key. The Circular Value Flower method presented in this book is a wonderful example of collaborating, being open to making connections and listening to each other's story. The book demonstrates that a circular neighbourhood can become a reality, and in the process contribute to a green, sustainable future for us all.

Mariska Joustra
Circular economy expert Milieu Centraal

Introduction

Why This Book?

In response to global climate goals and scarcity of resources, scientists are calling for measures to alter the current linear ways of production and to switch to a circular economy. The Dutch government is therefore advocating full circularity by 2050, which means seeing waste as a resource for new applications and as a result eliminating the use of even more non-renewable materials. In addition, the goal is to be energy-neutral in 2050 and in the meantime make our living environment climate-adaptive, nature-inclusive and biodiverse. It is a major task to structurally change existing patterns that are linked to the linear economy, and which in many cases are at the root of the current crises. The government formulates sustainability policies and citizens are also challenged on their behaviour and encouraged, for example, to separate waste, replace paving with plants, turn down the heating or take shorter showers. In our opinion, sustainable circular solutions would also benefit from a collective and systemic approach at the level of the neighbourhood or district, where a local community is central, in between the scale of the state and the individual. The introduction of the new Environment and Planning Act (Omgevingswet) in January 2023 will create more room for citizens to give direction to urban processes and projects themselves. At the same time, this new law, which links the physical and social domains, will have a significant impact on the work processes of government authorities and professionals working in spatial planning.

The above developments prompted us as spatial designers – an urban designer and an architect – active in the area of sustainable community development to investigate the possibilities for closing material and operational resource cycles at the local level and to develop a method to allow citizens, authorities and designers to jointly realize multiple value in neighbourhoods and districts. This study was conducted within the framework of the academic research programme Ontwerp & Overheid (Design & Government) at Delft University of Technology, Eindhoven University of Technology and Wageningen University, and led to the publication of this book.

We analyzed seven circular community initiatives in the Netherlands that focus on closing one or more types of resource cycles locally, for instance water, energy, nutrients and materials (including building materials) from the bio-based and technical cycles. The analysis was carried out using the Circular Value Flower method. This is a method of analysis and design that we developed during the research in order to unravel the integral processes that are needed to create valuable circular interventions at the scale of the neighbourhood or district. By means of this method, we have mapped out in an integral and transparent way the relationship between the circular ambitions of the initiators, their enabling capital, the necessary collaborations, the spatial interventions and the value creation realized within the physical living environment.

An increasing number of residents and local businesses are already taking responsibility for closing resource cycles in their own neighbourhood or district. For instance, we see neighbourhoods that are self-sufficient through collectively generated energy, neighbourhoods that filter grey water (waste water from kitchen and shower use) with helophyte filters in courtyard gardens, and neighbourhoods where organic and residual waste is reused to a high degree through their own resources station. These circular pioneers seem to be driven by the ambition to contribute to a sustainable society and they try to find answers with their initiatives to challenges such as the climate crisis, scarce and increasingly expensive raw materials, decreasing biodiversity and growing inequality. Many initiatives show that citizens are more than capable of organizing themselves, entering into necessary collaborations and achieving added value in their living environment by means of creative solutions. At the same time, the initiatives reveal the complexity of the design and development processes involved in closing resource cycles locally. After all, who is responsible for the development of new circular systems at a neighbourhood level? How do you work together with other stakeholders to achieve your ambitions? And what interests are at stake in the physical integration of these systems into the living environment, both in the public and the private domain?

In this book, we hope to demonstrate that the Circular Value Flower method, an insightful means of analysis, has great potential for facilitating bottom-up co-creation processes within circular community development. This book is therefore not only written for other design professionals, but is also of particular interest to ambitious citizens and municipalities who are engaged in closing material cycles at the neighbourhood level and who have the ambition to let valuable communities flourish together.

The Transition to a Circular Economy

The call to change our current economic model to a circular economy is echoed in many official policy documents at national, regional and local level. It means that we need to convert the current linear production chains of 'raw-material use – product – waste' into closed cycles in which waste and unnecessary use of raw materials are prevented. This process distinguishes between cycles of bio-based regenerative materials, such as wood and natural fibres, which can eventually be reabsorbed by the natural ecosystem, and cycles of finite technical materials, such as oil products (plastics), cement and steel, which can be reused through circular design strategies and circulate endlessly in the production system as a result.[1]

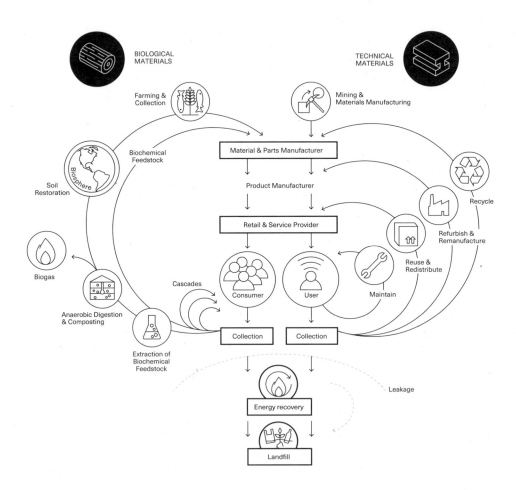

The butterfly diagram (based on Ellen MacArthur 2012)

1 Ellen MacArthur Foundation 2012; Ghisellini et al. 2016; Pomponi & Moncaster 2017
2 Netherlands Environmental Assessment Agency 2019

In order to close both of these raw-material cycles, the Netherlands Environmental Assessment Agency (PBL) uses the so-called R-Ladder[2], a cascade system of circular strategies, including design strategies. 'The higher a strategy is on the R-Ladder, the more circular it is.' The R-ladder can be summarized in the three steps of 'reduce, re-use and recycle':

- Reduce – At the top of the ladder is reducing consumption and production and making and using products in a smarter way.
- Re-use – In the middle is extending the life of products and components.
- Recycle – At the bottom is the useful recovery of materials that would otherwise go to landfill.

Circular economy

#	Strategy	Description	Category
10	Refuse	preventing the use of new materials/resources	smarter product use and manufacture
9	Reduce	reducing the use of new resources	
8	Rethink	(re)designing a product with circularity as a starting point	
7	Re-use	re-using a product with circularity as a starting point	extend lifespan of product and its parts
6	Repair	maintaining and repairing to prolong service life	
5	Refurbish	restoring and updating a product	
4	Remanufacture	making a new product from secondary materials	
3	Repurpose	re-using a product with different purpose/function	
2	Recycle	processing from product to resource and reuse	useful application of materials
1	Recover	recovering energy from materials	

Linear economy

The R-ladder (based on Netherlands Environmental Assessment Agency 2019)

The Transition to a Circular Economy

In addition to the categorization of the various 'solid' material flows in the bio-based and technical cycles, used in buildings, infrastructure, equipment, product packaging and other consumer goods, three daily 'flowing' operational resource cycles are distinguished within the built environment: water, nutrients and energy. These cycles are often referred to by scientists as a 'nexus' and are crucial for survival within the built environment. Particularly in relation to community development, there is a growing awareness of the need for a circular approach 'that enables local interactions between water, food and energy cycles, taking into account the synergies and trade-offs that arise from managing these three resources.'[3]

In the Netherlands, large utility companies and central systems take care of the transport of the flowing resources, which in most cases are currently totally disconnected from natural ecosystems. For example, relatively clean rainwater is transported in large quantities to the sewers, where it is mixed with grey and black waste water. Valuable nutrients in black waste water, which could easily be recovered locally and used to nourish people, animals, plants and trees, travel long distances to central waste-water treatment plants. With regard to energy production and supply, geopolitical tensions are causing rising prices and stagnation of renewable energy production.
In short, where we have seen large-scale centralized utilities as achievements for years, we are beginning to realize that considerable value is actually lost with these utilities, and that they make us vulnerable and dependent. Conversely, decentralized closing and connecting the various operational cycles has the potential to make the built environment function as a resilient ecosystem at the scale of the neighbourhood or district. For instance, by fertilizing gardens or parks with bokashi (fermented vegetable, fruit and garden waste) produced in the neighbourhood, and harvesting home-grown food or collecting rainwater in reed ponds within the public space. The central idea here is that human activity is inextricably linked to natural ecosystems and cannot be seen as separate from them.[4] In addition to closing resource cycles, when designing or redesigning the urban fabric we will therefore also have to focus on increasing biodiversity through nature-inclusive construction and making the urban infrastructure climate-adaptive. This will enable the built environment to cope with the consequences of climate change, such as flooding and heat stress.

We do not see circularity as an end in itself, but rather as a means to achieve a sustainable living environment. 'Sustainability is a state of a complex, dynamic system. In this state, a system can continue to flourish resiliently, in harmony, without requiring inputs from outside the system boundaries.'[5] In a sustainable economic system, all economic activities remain within the limits set by planet Earth, while contributing to the provision of sufficient shelter, food and well-being for all. Raworth (2017) calls this economic zone the 'doughnut', where the ecological ceiling and the social foundation represent the limits of the economic system and provide an indication to stay within the support capacity of the Earth's ecosystems. The small scale of neighbourhoods, districts and villages seems to be a good basis for circular initiatives. The system boundaries of, for example, a closed water or material cycle and the associated responsibilities for its development and maintenance are manageable and tangible for the people who live there. In addition, the impact of circular initiatives translates very directly into visible value for the neighbourhood, as the examples presented here will demonstrate.

We foresee that the trend of circular community development will continue, and this will bring about major changes in spatial planning, urban and architectural design and the associated development processes. The circular transition is often presented as a technological task, while at the same time it is extremely closely linked to social, organizational and institutional issues. It is precisely this lack of an integrated approach that raises many questions about design processes, the necessary knowledge and skills, responsibility and division of tasks. Closing the various resource cycles locally has the potential to add significant value to the natural and built environment, but it depends on a systemic approach; solutions need to be taken into account in a coherent way, in the same way as within a natural ecosystem.

In short, such a radical transition requires a different organization of the associated design and development processes, in which citizens play a central role and already have or can develop their own knowledge to influence their own actions. In addition to legislation and regulations at the national and international level, collective forms of local organization, with a greater and more active role for citizens and businesses, will be indispensable. As a design tool, the Circular Value Flower method offers a practical guide for these driven circular community developers.

3 Reinhard et. al. 2017
4 Koefoed 2019
5 Bosschaert 2022

Citizens in Action in Their Own Neighbourhood

All over the world, citizens are demanding authority, involvement and responsibility for the development and management of their own neighbourhood or district. This development offers significant opportunities for jointly closing resource cycles. In non-Western countries, developments such as self-building houses with second-hand construction materials and cooking on biogas from organic waste collected in the neighbourhood are often driven by an existing culture of community life, the absence of government and economic necessity. The context of Dutch initiatives is different, since the government has a greater influence on the living environment and facilities are often centrally organized, but here too initiatives often arise from the wish for a stronger community life. In many cases, citizens act out of idealism to jointly realize a sustainable, nature-inclusive or alternative way of living and working. Current crises, such as in housing and energy, are fuelling enthusiasm for collective residential forms or local energy systems even more.

The district or neighbourhood is increasingly seen, not only by citizens but also by policymakers, as the level of scale where integrated answers can be provided to complex topical issues such as the circular economy, energy transition, inequality or well-being. In the urban development of the 1960s and 1970s, the neighbourhood approach took a central position in Dutch planning policies, but due to emerging trends of digitalization, globalization, larger social networks, better infrastructural connections and the arrival of large-scale commercial parties (liberalization), the relationship between citizens and neighbourhoods weakened in the decades that followed.[6] In light of the transition to a sustainable society, the development of technical and spatial solutions at the collective scale of the neighbourhood or district is important as a link between central and individual systems.[7]

The renewed focus on the local as a solution to global problems – think global, act local – can be traced back, on the one hand, to the activation of the empowered citizens who can organize themselves more easily thanks to new digital opportunities. However, social tasks that were previously the responsibility of the state are being shifted to citizens. This is often based on a rhetoric that emphasizes 'we', 'together' and 'local', for instance 'participation society' in the Netherlands or 'Big Localism' in the UK. It remains to be seen, of course, whether individual citizens are able and willing to take on these responsibilities.[8] Criticism focuses on the fact that calling on the creativity, time and power of citizens is not easy for all citizens, which means that initiating and participating in collective initiatives is not possible for everyone.[9] If a small group of residents develops an initiative using their time, energy and resources, without the majority of the other residents being informed and given the opportunity to contribute, this undermines democratic legitimacy and leads to the exclusion of those citizens who are not self-reliant.[10]

6 Majoor & Smit 2019, pp. 31-32
7 Hughes & Hoffmann 2020
8 Davoudi & Madanipour 2015
9 Uitermark 2015
10 Meijer 2014; De Bruin 2017

In today's network society, a world of many alliances and forms of collaboration, governments (ranging from the state to municipalities) relate differently to citizens, companies and fellow government bodies than in the past.
In more and more domains, hierarchical, often vertical structures are making way for more horizontal connections, and the dynamics between such relationships are more networked than before. Empowered citizens organize themselves and find each other in temporary alliances related to specific themes. These networks are captured powerfully in terms such as the 'energetic society'[11] or the 'do democracy'[12]. These alliances negotiate with each other concerning the direction and the measures to be taken, and initiate local projects and experiments.[13]

The government continues to play a role in such networks and alliances, especially at the municipal level, where many responsibilities have been transferred due to the increasing shift of public tasks from the central to the local level of scale since the 1990s. This institutional change has been given various names in the professional literature: one frequently used term is network governance, for example. Although the debate on the pros and cons of this form of governance is still in full swing, there are indications that it can respond better than the classic, hierarchical 'top-down' approach to the social pluriformity and dynamics described above. Network governance enables policymakers to deal better with the increasingly blurred boundaries between different policy areas, and as a result to cope with the complexity of the transition to a sustainable society.[14]

Public-private partnerships have long been an interesting way of balancing the ever-increasing costs of public affairs between government and the market. Governments also increasingly see a role for citizens as the drivers of social change.[15] In order to control shrinking budgets and rising costs, governments have followed the private market's lead and switched to market and management-oriented thinking (generally referred to as New Public Management, introduced in the UK in 1991). Terms such as market forces, decentralization, competition and performance formed the new management terminology here, where efficiency and effectiveness prevailed in the execution of public tasks. In practice, this leads to financial values being considered more important than cultural, ecological or social values in the assessment of plans or processes. In recent years, this thinking has changed and the realization of 'public value' has been named as the highest goal of government action, referred to as New Public Governance.[16]

10 Meijer 2014; De Bruin 2017
11 Hajer 2011
12 Van de Wijdeven 2012
13 Evans et al. 2016
14 See, for example, Hajer 2009; Klijn & Koppenjan 2015
15 Uitermark 2015
16 Bekkers & Tummers 2018; Kuitert 2021

Partnerships between public authorities, private parties, individual and organized citizens and knowledge institutes (often referred to as the 'quadruple helix')[17] are seen as essential to jointly tackle tasks that are complex both in terms of organization and content on an urban scale. The question is, of course, whether a changing playing field will also lead to a level playing field where all parties are at the table on an equal footing. In practice, this is questionable because the government tends to 'monopolize or market the public good rather than invest in active citizenship in the public domain.[18] The government, market parties and citizens will all have to define or redefine and master these new roles. The challenge of achieving fruitful collaboration between the parties of the 'quadruple helix' requires not only active citizens but also efforts on the part of the government. 'Conditions must be created, space made, rules bent, or existing blocking institutions dismantled.'[19]
The Circular Value Flower method offers explicit opportunities to take multiple value creation as a starting point within a neighbourhood development and to give the interests of different parties a place.

17 Carayannis & Campbell 2010
18 Soeterbroek 2015, p. 32
19 Van der Schot 2016

The New Environment and Planning Act

The way in which neighbourhoods and districts and developments are created is changing and will change even more with the arrival of the forthcoming Environment and Planning Act (Omgevingswet). This new law, which is expected to come into force in 2023, offers explicit scope for citizens' initiatives and local commissioning. In anticipation of it coming into force, a number of pilot projects are currently underway to see how this law works in practice, for instance the area development project in the Binckhorst (The Hague). Where previously governments, in collaboration with spatial designers and project developers, were responsible for the design and quality of public space and the management of utilities, the new Environment and Planning Act gives local residents more freedom and also responsibilities to design their living environment sustainably. In the future, who decides which values will be developed locally?

The new Environment and Planning Act offers opportunities for the changing playing field in two ways. Firstly, a decree stipulates that public participation must take place at an early stage in the development of an environmental vision. Citizens, businesses, social organizations and other administrative bodies must be involved in the preparation of a spatial-development vision, and the results must be made visible in the process. Secondly, it will be easier for citizens, businesses and organizations to submit private initiatives and get them approved.

For this purpose, the system of detailed permits has been abandoned in favour of more general rules for the assessment of ideas.[20] This creates a playing field where public values, decision-making and ownership are not only secured through representative democracy, but where space is created for other forms of involvement. A participation ladder[21] indicates different forms of possible involvement of parties other than the government, ranging from informing and consulting, to deciding and acting together and ultimately self-organization. The last three categories in particular can be at odds with the democratic legitimacy mentioned earlier. Representative democracy safeguards this democratic legitimacy: the general public elect representatives – politicians – who make policies that are implemented by government bodies. These elected representatives of the people and the public bodies therefore serve the general public interest. Other groups, citizens, businesses or civil society often serve local or specific objectives concerning a particular issue or theme. For example, citizens join forces to design a square or develop the programme in a community centre, initiatives that may only be actively supported by a select group of people (but for which there may be a great deal of support). However, not everyone votes, so our representative democracy also represents only part of the population. David van Reybrouck (2016) therefore argues for other forms in order to obtain democratic legitimacy, such as direct or participatory democracy. Other forms of democracy do not

---

20 See also https://www.rijksoverheid.nl/onderwerpen/omgevingswet
21 See Arnstein 1969; Wilcox 1994

necessarily replace representative democracy, but can actually strengthen it. Citizens seem to be open to such new roles in urban development, as demonstrated by the recent city monitor of the city of Amsterdam: 'Do not decide for us. Do it together with us and make us co-owners. We have so many valuable networks in our neighbourhoods that are able to take responsibility.'[22]

Degree of citizen participation

8	Citizen Control	Citizen Control
7	Delegated Power	
6	Partnership	
5	Placation	Tokenism
4	Consultation	
3	Informing	
2	Therapy	Nonparticipation
1	Manipulation	

The participation ladder (Arnstein 1969)

---

22 Stadsmonitor Amsterdam 2020, p. 6

The Selected Cases

The central question in this study – how citizens can create added value in their neighbourhood by closing resource cycles as locally as possible – is answered by an analysis of seven circular community initiatives. Practical examples were chosen because by studying the initiatives in their geographical and spatial contexts, insights can be gained into the integral approach taken by the initiators and their relationships and interactions with other parties.

The seven cases studied, citizens' initiatives aimed at closing one or more resource cycles, originated within the changing playing field described above. The cases were selected on the basis of five criteria:

1. Circularity: a project was set up or a solution was sought to close one or more of the following resource flows: water, energy, nutrients, bio-based and technical materials.
2. Residents' or cooperative initiative: although collaboration between the various parties (market, government, knowledge institutions, civil society/citizens and designers) occurs in many initiatives, only initiatives in which citizens or a neighbourhood cooperative played a decisive role in the initiation phase were considered, in order to be certain of meeting the criterion that it is a local initiative.
3. Local scale level: it concerns a recent initiative that has the ambition to have an impact at neighbourhood or district level through jointly initiated and developed interventions.
4. Spatial-visual implications: the interventions should be visible in the physical space.
5. Innovative organizational forms for the design and/or development process: the initiating citizens collaborate intensively with authorities, businesses, designers and/or knowledge institutions.

In addition, the selection of these practical examples also took into account the representation of both new and existing neighbourhoods, the geographical distribution within the Netherlands and the representation of each resource cycle, so that all the cycles are covered. After applying these selection criteria to a longlist of circular initiatives already realized or under development in the Netherlands, the following seven initiatives were selected, which together provide a valuable overview of circular community initiatives from which lessons can be learned.

The selected cases are as follows:

Afrikaanderwijk Coöperatie, Afrikaanderwijk, Rotterdam

The Afrikaanderwijk Coöperatie has taken over the handling of the waste from the Afrikaander market from the Rotterdam municipality. In this way, waste is processed in separate streams, a number of residents have been helped to find jobs and the quality of life in the neighbourhood has improved.

I'M Binck, Binckhorst, Den Haag

The Binckhorst is a redevelopment area in The Hague that has been designated by the municipality as a testing ground for innovation and creativity. I'M Binck – a local initiative set up by mobile project office OpTrek – attempts to give topical themes such as energy transition, climate adaptation, nature-inclusive construction, and giving the circular economy a place in the area and bringing it to the attention of the businesses by building up a large network.

Schoonschip, Buiksloterham, Amsterdam

In 2008, a number of residents took the initiative to develop a floating residential area in Amsterdam, for which, after a two-year search, a suitable location was found on the Johan van Hasselt Canal. The ambition was to create a district that is as self-sufficient as possible, where the houseboats are made of sustainable materials, energy is generated locally and exchanged via a smart grid, and sewage-water processing, water collection and use are dealt with intelligently.

DeBlauweWij(k)Economie, Spijkerkwartier, Arnhem

In the Spijkerkwartier in Arnhem, a number of citizens have started a neighbourhood initiative for collective solar panels: Spijkerenergie. This initiative has since grown into a network of different community initiatives, all of which focus on creating a sustainable local neighbourhood economy based on values already present in the neighbourhood. The BuurtGroenBedrijf, for example, focuses on a nature-inclusive, clean and attractive living environment, and the BuurtBaanBureau helps local residents who are unemployed to find work. These initiatives are united in deBlauweWij(k)Economie foundation.

Plant je Vlag - IEWAN, Vossenpels, Nijmegen

Initiatiefgroep Ecologisch Woonproject Arnhem Nijmegen (IEWAN) has developed the largest straw-built residential complex in the Netherlands in the Vossenpels district of Nijmegen, with room for different types of households. The special feature of the project, which is now known as Strowijk (Straw District), is that it is social housing and is based on ecological principles on several levels.

Delfshaven Coöperatie, Bospolder Tussendijken (BoTu), Rotterdam

The Delfshaven Coöperatie aims to explore new partnerships between residents and public and private parties in order to bring about sustainable redevelopment of the Bospolder Tussendijken (BoTu) district in Rotterdam. The focus here is emphatically on creating added value on the spot. The district installation company WijkEnergieWerkt is also located in BoTu. It is a social enterprise that is not only accelerating the energy transition in the neighbourhood, but also trains and employs local residents to do so. WijkEnergieWerkt works together with the Delfshaven Coöperatie.

Heliport Groen, Heliport, Rotterdam

By means of a citizens' initiative, residents have created a more pleasant living environment in Heliport's collectively used inner courtyard, with consideration for biodiversity and climate adaptation. The project was designed and implemented in collaboration with Stichting Tussentuin and the municipality of Rotterdam.

Reader's Guide

After this introduction, an explanation of the Circular Value Flower method follows in chapter 2. This method provides a framework for analyzing the practical examples discussed in the third chapter. Chapter 4 then discusses the insights gained from the analysis of the cases, after which we conclude the book with a number of lessons that we believe are important in accerelating the transition to a sustainable and therefore also circular living environment.

The Circular Value Flower

The Circular Value Flower

To provide insight into the complex process of collaboratively closing resource cycles at neighbourhood or district level, we developed a conceptual analysis model and associated design method: the Circular Value Flower. The Circular Value Flower method supports a systematic analysis of initiatives by showing in different layers how closing resource cycles at the local scale can ultimately result in multiple value creation.

Increasingly, urban development is expressed not only in terms of money but also includes the creation of values in a broader societal sense. In the Netherlands, in addition to gross domestic product, which is the measure of economic development, aspects such as well-being and living environment are now included in the overall picture of the state of the country. A country like Iceland has gone a step further, and measures the state of the country in 39 indicators, of which gross domestic product is just one. The others are, for example, CO_2 emissions, education and housing.[1] The call for a different valuation of our society other than purely in economic value is fuelled by the climate crisis; the current level of production and consumption on which economies run depletes the earth and therefore our living environment. A circular economy, as discussed in Chapter 1, operates within the boundaries set by the planetary ecosystems. Driven by stricter environmental standards, future economic activities will increasingly focus on multiple value creation, where economic, ecological and social values are in balance. Business models will then more often consist of a combination of different values, with long-term profit, reciprocity and ecologically responsible and socially just aspects on an equal footing with each other. All the stakeholders benefit in such a situation.[2] The transition to a 'well-being economy' requires not only a different attitude towards production and consumption, but also another organizational framework. Here, collaboration between the various parties is essential to create values on different themes in such a way that they collectively lead to a sustainable system.[3] Central to this framework are circular systems that operate in conjunction and at different scales, ranging from local to global. Urban policy, design and governance play an important role in multiple value creation, especially at the scale of the neighbourhood.

The tricky thing is that some values, for instance economic and ecological, are easier to translate into numbers than values relating to 'softer' aspects such as well-being and liveability. For example, mapping out incomes, employment or CO_2 and nitrogen emissions may be easy in numbers, but cultural and aesthetic values are not. In order to make informed decisions within policymaking or design processes, transparent and balanced consideration of the different values is crucial. Many methodologies have already been developed to achieve balanced consideration. These methods juxtapose quantitative and qualitative values, serving as tools for analysis or vision development.

A number of these methodologies – Waardenbenadering Leefomgeving (Living Environment Values Approach), Doughnut model, Thriving City Index, The Just City Index[4] – have been reviewed for their usefulness for analyzing circular neighbourhood initiatives and identifying the links between resource cycles, spatial impact and multiple value creation. These methodologies provide qualitative (Waardenbenadering and The Just City Index) or quantitative (Doughnut Model and Thriving City Index) insights into value creation at a local scale (and in the case of the Doughnut Model on a global scale as well), where in addition to economic values, there is also a major role for social, cultural and ecological values.

Theoretically, the result of an integrated values approach within urban development should be increased liveability in the neighbourhood or district. Liveability is a difficult concept to define, and is prone to subjective interpretations, but in general, liveability is described as a multiplicity of values and experiences from everyday life in a given spatial context (a place) that impact both the individual and the community.[5] Or in a nutshell, liveability is the quality of the relationship between people and their spatial environment. This includes both physical infrastructure (schools, parks, roads and housing) and the interrelationship of residents and users with this infrastructure and each other.[6] The 'Place and Happiness Survey'[7] captures the essence of a liveable neighbourhood in five categories:

1. Physical and economic security;
2. Basic services (schools, houses et etcetera);
3. Leadership;
4. Openness (tolerance, inclusiveness between different groups of residents); and
5. Aesthetics (physical beauty, culture, and so on).

These categories indicate that the presence of basic infrastructure alone is not enough for a pleasant living environment, but that it is primarily about the quality and interplay between spatial and social elements and their organization. Florida's research found that the very last item in his enumeration – 'a pleasant and attractive living environment' – is for residents one of the most important characteristics of a liveable neighbourhood.[8]

---

1 See, for example, OECD 2020
2 See, for example, Trebeck & Williams 2019; Raworth 2017
3 Fotino et al. 2018
4 See www.waardenbenadering.nl; https://doughnuteconomics.org/news/48; www.thrivingcitiesindex.org; www.designforthejustcity.org
5 Lloyd et al. 2016
6 Van Dorst 2012
7 Florida 2008
8 Ibid., p. 173

The models mentioned above indicate that in addition to economic value, social, ecological and cultural values are also important to develop sustainable and fair neighbourhoods and cities. In addition, Florida (2008) argues that aesthetic value should also be taken into account within local value-creation processes. That is why the following five values – aesthetic, social, economic, ecological and cultural – are included in our analysis model, the Circular Value Flower.

Layers of the Circular Value Flower

The Circular Value Flower is composed of five layers, where the initiators with their ambition(s) occupy a central position in the graphic representation of the model. The first layer shows the potential of activating capital that is present or needed within the community, followed by the different resource cycles that initiatives focus on in the second layer: water, energy, nutrients, and biological and technical materials. The third layer features the possible parties with which the initiators may enter into relationships to realize their ambitions: public bodies, private businesses, civic society (NGOs, interest groups), designers and knowledge institutes. The fourth layer focuses on the initiatives' potential spatial interventions and are divided into buildings, infrastructure, public space, gardens and urban objects. The outer layer is formed by the values discussed earlier: social, economic, ecological, aesthetic and cultural values.

The Circular Value Flower with its five layers provides the framework for analysis of the cases. For each case study, we have described what the initiators' ambition was for the neighbourhood with regard to implementing or closing a resource cycle, what their activating capital was, with whom they collaborated, what spatial/physical impact circular interventions had, and what values these interventions generated for the neighbourhood and its residents.

Community Ambitions and Activating Capital

One or more ambitions underlie the initiators' ideas and plans. These ambitions are often specific to the project and context but can generally be categorized under a number of overarching themes, such as 'sustainability' (restoring and reproducing way of dealing with life and the living environment), 'democratic' (transparency, broad support and high level of participation), 'well-being' (healthy, safe and pleasant community and living environment), and 'equality' (equal opportunities for all).

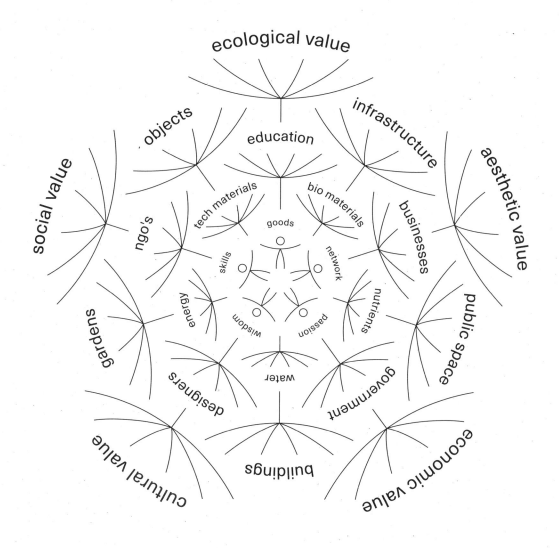

Layers of the Circular Value Flower

In addition to having, formulating and communicating ambitions on one or more themes, the extent to which activating capital is present among the initiators and in the community is extremely important for achieving these ambitions. Having knowledge about resource cycles and the current and possible alternative system (of governance) in which they are produced is important. Knowledge is part of the broader concept of 'wisdom', which can also include other insights passed down from generation to generation.
By extension, skills such as communication, organizational and perseverance strengths are needed to turn formulated ambitions into actual implementation of solutions. Being able to tap into the social fabric of the neighbourhood is also indispensable, as are assets, financial and otherwise. Lastly, passion combined with a sense of urgency forms the basis for the motivation behind launching initiatives themselves in order to realize added value in the neighbourhood.

Collaboration and Process Methods

Local initiatives have been selected if they are an initiative by citizens or a local organization and therefore not initiated by the government or an external private company. Of course, this does not alter the fact that in many cases parties such as the city council, businesses and knowledge institutions have been partners within circular initiatives. Research was conducted into the kind of collaborations with officials, businesses (local or otherwise) and knowledge institutions, considering in particular the relationships between them and the degree of control and decision-making power. The role of the designer, if involved in projects, was also included in the analysis. It was interesting to see who the designer's commissioning client was, what the relationships were between client and contractor, and whether the designer's role was different from their role in 'traditional' projects. The analysis therefore focuses specifically on the perspective of the initiators, often pioneers or front runners, who in many cases started the initiatives on the basis of a personal ambition. Gaining insight into the problem areas in the various circular initiatives can help improve the value-creation processes of future initiatives. The analysis therefore aims to highlight the perspective of the front runners and learn from their experiences.

Resource Cycles

In summary, the analysis recognizes the following resource flows or 'cycles': water, energy, nutrients, and biological and technical materials.

Physical Development

This layer looks at how the initiatives translate spatially, for example into new plant beds in public spaces or the construction of resource stations for local waste treatment. What are the implications for the physical environment, and how and where are the resource cycles implemented in the neighbourhood or district? The following elements are distinguished here: buildings, public space, gardens, urban objects and infrastructural elements.

Values

In our current value system, value often refers only to economic value, but in the context of neighbourhood development this is too narrow a definition, as explained above. That is why the outer layer of the Circular Value Flower identifies five values: ecological, social, cultural, economic and aesthetic, which provide a qualitative analysis of whether they are increased by the initiative.

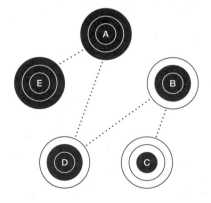

Layered onion diagram

For three of the five layers of the Circular Value Flower – parties, resource cycles and values – the results of the analysis are shown in a separate layered onion diagram. These diagrams indicate the extent to which a particular party, resource or value occurs with a qualitative indication, visually represented by colouring the rings of a sphere, where an open sphere represents 'nothing' or 'none', one ring represents 'to a limited extent' and two rings means 'to a large extent'. In addition, the dotted lines show the interconnections or relationships between the different elements.

The Value Flower Field Map

The research into the various neighbourhood initiatives was based primarily on documentation that was available about the various projects, neighbourhoods and initiatives. These documents consisted of websites, policy documents, newspaper articles, vision and design plans, and reports. For a full list of documents consulted by case, see 156-157.

As a second approach, interviews were conducted with stakeholders, according to a semi-structured questionnaire based on the layers of the Circular Value Flower. This allowed the case studies to be analyzed following the same pattern each time, while also leaving room for sharing more informal facts that bring the context of a case study to life. For each case, one or more initiators and one of the designers (where present) were interviewed, in some cases several times.

The cases were then expressed in words and images, based on the layers of the Circular Value Flower. Prior to the study, one of the aims was to present in clear diagrams the complex integral process by which neighbourhood initiatives are developed. Two types of diagrams were developed for this purpose. The first diagram is an interpretation of the Circular Value Flower as a whole in a Value Flower Field Map. Here, the various layers of the Circular Value Flower and their interrelationships are depicted in a single visual overview. The map shows physical developments on the central vertical axis, with the spatial context of the neighbourhood at the bottom and spatial interventions above. In addition, the process from initiative to value creation is represented as a cyclical process through the use of different icons that correspond to the layers of the Circular Value Flower.

The second diagram shows the quality of the elements of a specific case by layer. For three of the five layers of the Circular Value Flower – parties, resource cycles and values – the results of the analysis are shown in a separate layered onion diagram. These diagrams indicate the extent to which a particular party, resource or value occurs with a qualitative indication, visually represented by colouring the rings of a sphere, where an open sphere represents 'nothing' or 'none', one ring represents 'to a limited extent' and two rings means 'to a large extent' (see Figure p. 31). In addition, the dotted lines show the interconnections or relationships between the different elements.

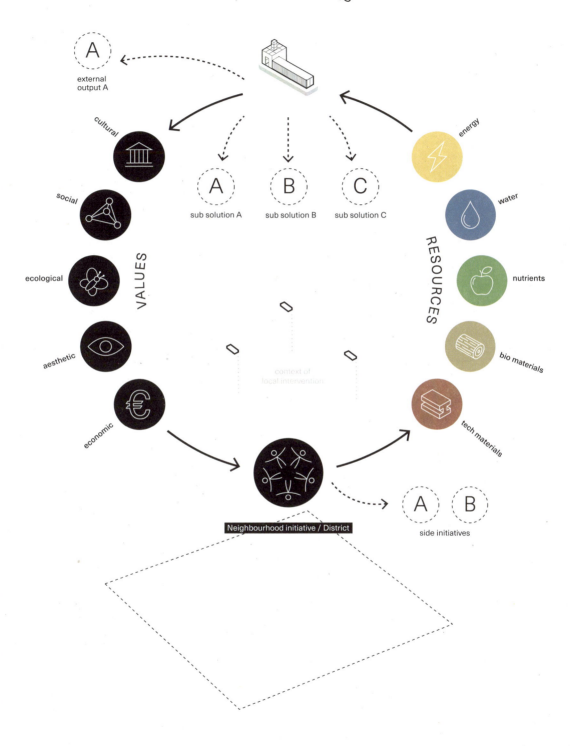

The Value Flower Field Map

Choices Made

The Cases Observed

As a limitation, the small number of practical examples studied can be mentioned, while by now so many good circular examples can be found in the Netherlands. For this book, we have limited ourselves to the selection we made. We see the publication of this book as the start of further research into initiatives and we like collecting other good examples. On the website *www.circularcommunity.org*, we aim to share as many circular neighbourhood and district initiatives as possible to provide inspiration. If you would like to share your initiative or project with our online community, please *contact info@circularcommunity.org*.

The Interviews Held

The choice was made in this research to analyze the case studies from the perspective of the initiators, i.e., from the perspective of citizens (generally operating in organized form). Interviews were therefore mainly conducted with them and with designers who were involved in the process or processes. So although the seven neighbourhoods studied here have provided a wealth of information, the voice of other parties such as council officials or businesses is only present in the background. If anything, the representation of the initiatives provides a somewhat one-sided picture here and there.

Comparison of Value Methodologies

The value methodologies discussed at the beginning of this chapter are not compared with each other, but serve only to understand what values are important for analyzing and creating added value at the neighbourhood level of scale. The original ambition of the research team was to provide a quantitative analysis of the resource flows and value created in the neighbourhood, in addition to the qualitative perspective. Due to a lack of available data on this aspect, the quantitative side has been given limited consideration in this study. A follow-up will focus further on this area.

Definitions Used

In the theoretical section – Chapters 1 and 2 – we make extensive use of definitions and views formulated by scientists. However, scientists often disagree or have their own particular emphasis. We have tried to make a good choice here by sometimes showing different points of view, or using the most common definitions, but have also made a subjective selection so that precisely the definitions that support our mission – accelerating the transition to a sustainable and just society – are used.

Missing Links within the Closed Resource Cycles

When can a neighbourhood-level solution actually be called circular? In this research study, most examples are strictly speaking not fully circular, i.e., links are missing to fully close a cycle at the neighbourhood or district level. However, we have nonetheless included these examples in the book, because each small step can help us learn how to achieve a fully circular built environment.

A second limitation in this study with regard to closing the various resource cycles is the lack of physical and spatial interpretation of the different components of an ideal closed value chain by resource type. Unanswered questions include: what is needed in spatial and physical terms in a neighbourhood to collect, store, distribute and finally use rainwater as flushing water for a toilet and to re-purify the grey water through a helophyte filter? And where are the opportunities for using design to add value in the neighbourhood by integrating resource cycles in the physical domain? We see refinement of the Circular Value Flower with a layer consisting of the different steps (collection, storage, distribution, use, feedback) of a closed cycle as a valuable future development.

Practical Examples

Afrikaanderwijk Coöperatie

Afrikaanderwijk, Rotterdam

The Afrikaanderwijk is located in Rotterdam South and is considered one of the Netherlands' first multicultural neighbourhoods. Over 9,000 people live around Afrikaanderplein, where the Afrikaander market takes place twice a week, attracting 15,000 people a day. The Afrikaanderwijk Coöperatie has taken over the collection of the market's waste from the city council through a 'Right to Challenge' initiative. As a result, waste is now collected separately throughout the day during market hours by workers from the neighbourhood, reducing litter and making the market and the neighbourhood cleaner. In this way, money flows remain local through 'insourcing'.

Collection of paper and cardboard by a neighbourhood cooperative employee

Ambitions

The Afrikaanderwijk Coöperatie was founded in 2013 with the aim of creating both economic and social value in the neighbourhood by initiating, stimulating and organizing local initiatives. The qualities already present in the neighbourhood, in its residents, businesses and the physical environment, are taken as the starting point for inclusive development. A number of initiatives aimed at creating local jobs have now been successfully developed: a transport bank, a bicycle bank, a cleaning company, a landscaping company, management and rental of 't Gemaal op Zuid – a community centre where cultural programmes have also found a home – a community kitchen and the community workspace.

In addition to these services, a circular initiative has been set up for processing waste from the Afrikaander market. In principle, the market traders are responsible for disposing of their own refuse, but an average of five cubic metres of waste is still left behind after a typical market day. The city council used to collect this waste as an unsorted residual stream at the end of the day.

Now that the Afrikaanderwijk Coöperatie has taken over waste collection, the waste is separated as much as possible and a minimum amount of residual waste is disposed of. As a result of the Afrikaanderwijk Coöperatie taking over this collection, several local residents have found jobs, the neighbourhood has become cleaner because litter is collected throughout the market day and waste is collected separately, some of it for reuse. It involves collaboration with Rotterdam waste-management company Renes.

Collaboration and Process Method

The Afrikaanderwijk Coöperatie is a network organization, whose members consist of different types of parties from the neighbourhood, such as residents, businesses, organizations and local NGOs. It collaborates with local and external partners in developing initiatives. To design the initiative of a circular market, a working group was set up in which, in addition to the cooperative and the city council, design bureau Superuse Studios was involved in thinking about local value creation from residual flows. Current procurement rules made it difficult to realize the shared ambition of the cooperative and the council – on-site waste separation by local workers. The 'Right to Challenge' instrument (see explanation) offered a solution. Collaboration with the city council was initially through a co-creative process, with three different council departments and the cooperative at the table as equal partners. The Right to Challenge construction changed this into a relationship of client (City of Rotterdam) and contractor (Afrikaanderwijk Coöperatie), which made the process more fragile. Although relations with individual officials were good, the innovative nature of the initiative clashed with the inflexibility of the system and the various departments that had to grant approval.

'We had a difficult relationship with the city council system, because everything we do is new. So you end up in a system that is very ordered and cannot handle exceptions well; it is also unable to deal with the flexibility of organizing in a neighbourhood. I find it difficult because I can't hold anyone accountable for this situation within the council because everyone runs up against the same system.' (Afrikaanderwijk Coöperatie)

In addition, spending and revenues for waste processing fall under different council departments, making it difficult to reconcile budgets. The revenue generated by separated waste (mainly paper and cardboard) does not yet make the business model viable for the cooperative.

'This is also because you are expected to make your business case financially sound according to the norms of the linear economic system. We should actually make those investments in a circular economy as a society, otherwise as a company you bear all the risks and are vulnerable.' (Afrikaanderwijk Coöperatie)

Twelve jobs have now been created at the market for the two market days a week, Wednesday and Saturday. Some of these places are filled by young people who have this as a part-time job. To be able to offer full-time jobs to their employees though, these workers are also deployed elsewhere.

Wholesalers and market traders are themselves important participants in this process as well. Market traders responded enthusiastically to opportunities for local processing and separation of waste, as long as they did not incur additional costs. Like every business, they have the responsibility to enter into their own waste contract, where financial considerations are decisive.

Design bureau Superuse Studios has been a partner of the cooperative and its predecessor Freehouse for more than a decade. They work together on projects, where they sometimes switch roles. For example, for a CityLab010 grant – a Rotterdam subsidy scheme that supports initiatives by city residents – Superuse Studios was the applicant and therefore the commissioning client of the neighbourhood cooperative, but for a grant from the Creative Industries Fund NL, it was the other way round. The knowledge and expertise brought in by Superuse Studios supports the initiatives of the neighbourhood cooperative. For instance, Superuse Studios is initiating and developing several spatial concepts together with the Afrikaanderwijk Coöperatie, such as the resources station being built on the market in 2022 and the initiative to create a green roof from discarded market crates. The latter is being experimented with on the roof of the Gemaal community centre.

In addition, the cooperative works intensively with the Willem de Kooning Academy. Students study opportunities for local value creation from market residual flows, which has already led to several prototypes. For example, jam was made from leftover fruit in collaboration with a local jam factory and a market trolley was developed consisting of plastic-bag litter.

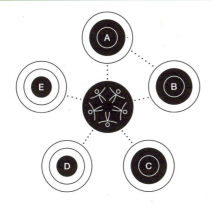

COLLABORATION

A Designers
B Government
C Businesses
D Ngo's
E Education

Process Method:
Right to Challenge

Right to Challenge is a form of democratic renewal that gives citizens in a neighbourhood or district the right to take over local government services if they think they can organize it differently or better themselves. This also means that organized citizens gain ownership or co-ownership and a say over local facilities, whereas previously the organization of these facilities was the responsibility of the local council. This policy instrument has been used for some time in the UK and found its way into Rotterdam local government policy under councillor De Jonge in 2014. It does require local organizations to submit a well-thought-out plan to the city council, which then approves it. These initiatives are generally within the organizational reach of residents, for instance developing collective vegetable gardens or a food forest.

'But if you really want to achieve something structurally and also really want to change the system, it really does become much more complex and you need to have people who want it, within the system as well. So a Right to Challenge is by no means easy and is certainly not for everyone. When it involves vulnerable neighbourhoods, it becomes even more difficult. Here in Rotterdam we have the system with the residents' initiatives, which is very accessible, but even that is often too complex for some people. And a Right to Challenge is a million times harder.' (Afrikaanderwijk Coöperatie)

Collection of paper and cardboard by a neighbourhood cooperative employee

Resource Cycles

The Afrikaander market is the third largest market in the Netherlands with some 280 stalls and 15,000 visitors a day. Although it is a more sustainable form of retail than shops, a market also produces a lot of residual waste: cardboard and paper, fruit and vegetable waste (the largest stream), and a variety of plastics. The plastic bags blowing away, for example, cause a lot of nuisance in the rest of the neighbourhood. Rather than seeing this solely as a problem, the Afrikaanderwijk Coöperatie recognized an opportunity here:

'We could also turn it round and see the market as a labour market rather than a waste market.' (Afrikaanderwijk Coöperatie).

That is why the circular market initiative starts with on-site separation of waste by local workers during market days, and then processing it in as circular a way as possible. High-value materials can flow back to the market. Subsequently, other materials could be processed into semi-finished products, such as compost, biogas, fibres that could be used for the paper and/or rope industry, and so on. For example, an experiment was carried out where pineapple skins were made into rope. An initiative was recently developed to use the disposable single-use plastic crates in which fruit and vegetables are transported as components for a green roof. The crates are placed side by side and filled with soil, plants and flowers. As a result, they form an affordable, self-made green roof. A green roof contributes to a building's insulation and climate adaptation by capturing and delaying rainwater runoff.

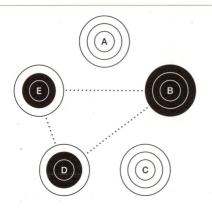

RESOURCE CYCLES

A Energy
B Nutrients
C Water
D Bio Materials
E Tech Materials

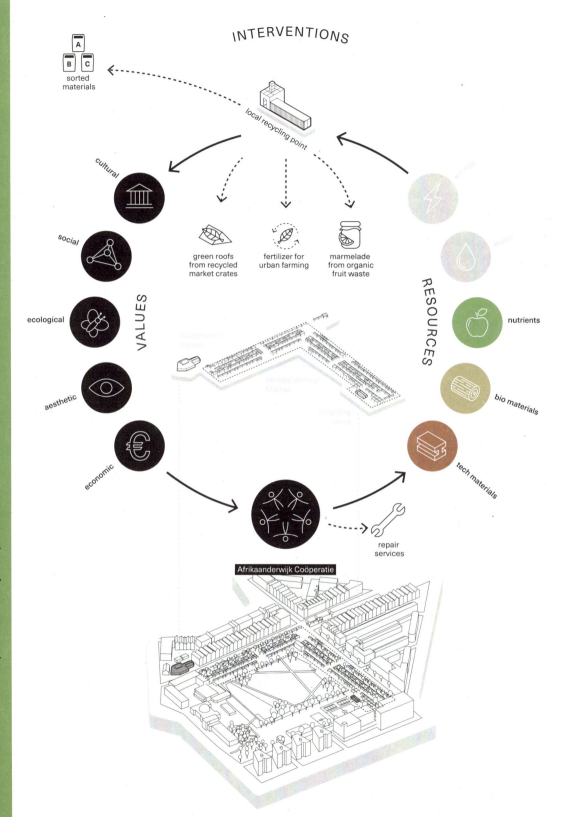

Physical Developments

A design was made by Superuse Studios for a resources station to be located at the market. Here, waste is separated on site and already partially processed on the days the market is in operation. Three phases have been designed for this circular station, with funding already secured for the first phase through CityLab 010. In addition to waste separation, the station includes a demonstration area, where examples of products made from residual waste will be displayed to raise awareness. Materials from residual flows are processed according to the cascading principle: firstly, reusing them in as high value a way as possible, and only then finding more low-value applications. The ultimate ambition is to create an iconic station where, besides collecting and separating waste, social functions such as a repair café, goods exchange, give-away shop or makerspace can also be included and where, in addition to market traders, local residents and businesses can use the station, several days a week. The definitive resources station is being built in the Afrikaanderwijk in 2022.

Resources station design by Superuse Studios

DIY green roof, made from used market crates

A physical location is not only convenient in terms of logistic flows. On-site processing of waste by local workers also contributes to the visibility and awareness of market traders and shoppers.

The initiative to use the plastic crates for a green roof is now being tested on the roof of the Gemaal, a community centre from which the Afrikaanderwijk Coöperatie also operates. If this proves successful, other roofs could also be provided with flowers and grasses in this way.

Work meeting at current resources station

Values

The added value of the work of the Afrikaanderwijk Coöperatie and specifically the initiatives relating to the circular Afrikaander market lies primarily in the financial and socio-cultural domain. The cooperative now employs 45 people, with 12 of them working at the market since January 2021.

'Out of 9,000 local residents this counts for very little, of course, but these people know other people who, as a result, also experience that working can be very different. Many people we work with have always been at the bottom of the labour-market ladder and are often not treated too well, and we are trying to do things very differently. There are people here who don't know anyone who has a job, so if you can change a few people in that situation, it has a big reach in raising awareness.' (Afrikaanderwijk Coöperatie)

This awareness-raising is realized not only in terms of employment, but also in the area of sustainability by visibly separating waste on market days.

'Raising awareness is extremely important. It is also one of the reasons we started cleaning during the day to show that there are 'real' people working to maintain the neighbourhood. Seeing the cleaner busy triggers people to keep the place cleaner themselves.' (Afrikaanderwijk Coöperatie)

In addition, by separating, reusing and recycling products and materials on site, circular market initiatives contribute to local and national sustainability ambitions. By providing positive impulses, the cooperative also hopes to overturn the negative perceptions that often prevail in the neighbourhood itself, but also about the neighbourhood. On the one hand, the initiatives contribute to financial strength, but also to a cleaner and therefore more attractive neighbourhood.

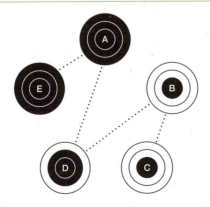

VALUES

A Social
B Ecological
C Aesthetic
D Cultural
E Economic

Conclusion

The aim of the Afrikaanderwijk Coöperatie is to make the Afrikaanderwijk and its residents more resilient by developing initiatives in co-creation with local businesses, residents and external partners such as the city council and experts, based on the local environment and the opportunities available there.

'We are creating a different way of working, another type of collaboration with the local government. Of course, as outsiders we don't have all the answers either, so I prefer to work closely with the city council. In co-creation. We pick out the people who understand and want to innovate. So in the area of innovative collaboration between local government and citizens, value is created.' (Afrikaanderwijk Coöperatie)

However, this collaboration does not come naturally (yet). Because the council is the one paying, the respective positions in the process are not equal: the Right to Challenge arrangement has replaced the previous collaboration based on equal positions with a classic client-contractor relationship.

'There is always an area of tension in this type of collaboration between wanting to co-create on an equal footing and the client-contractor relationship that is actually created by the financial flows.' (Afrikaanderwijk Coöperatie)

Exploring new value systems through pilot projects or experiments inherently carries the risk that things will turn out differently than imagined. Often, a pilot project or experiment is then dismissed as unsuccessful and people revert to the old system or the familiar way of doing things.

'But especially if people (in vulnerable positions) are part of the project, it is important to realize that you can't just run a little project that then stops, but that instead you need to try to change the system in a structural way. To develop a new model, you therefore don't so much need a short-term project, but rather a long-term process in which learning and exploration are seen as a valuable part of the journey.' (Afrikaanderwijk Coöperatie)

An experiment or pilot should be a structural component of a way of working in order to keep innovating, and not a temporary project carried out alongside the existing way of working. Structural system change actually needs that interaction with the existing system and time to allow innovations to grow to provide a sustainable alternative.

Subsequently, the permanence of these processes also depends on the involvement of both public and private individuals.

'Civil servants change jobs frequently; those positions are very volatile. So sometimes you have built up a bond and developed a process with certain people and then they leave and are replaced by people who have not gone through that whole preliminary process. And they look at the situation in a completely different way.' (Afrikaanderwijk Coöperatie)

Additionally, the city council is a many-headed monster.

'When the various departments are not aligned with each other, it is difficult to work with them.' (Superuse Studios).

Despite the laborious and obstinate nature of official decision-making, this case study shows that cooperative entrepreneurship in collaboration with local government can contribute a great deal to the economic and social development of a neighbourhood. That said, citizen participation, especially in vulnerable neighbourhoods, is not a given in such processes. How much time and energy can you expect from citizens who generally carry out these types of initiatives in their spare time?

The business model relating to the processing of the Afrikaander market waste demonstrates that closing resource cycles can pay off and, in addition to economic value, actually deliver social and ecological values.

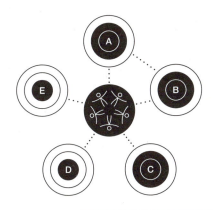

COLLABORATION

A Designers
B Government
C Businesses
D Ngo's
E Education

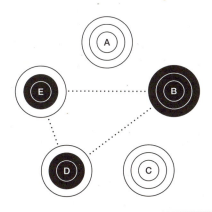

RESOURCE CYCLES

A Energy
B Nutrients
C Water
D Bio Materials
E Tech Materials

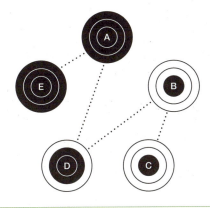

VALUES

A Social
B Ecological
C Aesthetic
D Cultural
E Economic

I'M Binck
The Binckhorst, The Hague

Planting trees and shrubs together on the CarWeide

The Binckhorst is a centrally located inner-city business park in The Hague that is being developed into a mixed residential, working and living area. In the original large-scale plans, all existing industrial buildings were due to be replaced by housing, but the financial crisis (2011) meant that these plans were abandoned.

The city council subsequently decided on an organic area-development approach based on the existing qualities and activities, and invited everyone to contribute ideas and invest. The area has been designated a testing ground for innovation and creativity and provides an ideal opportunity for testing the new Environment and Planning Act.

For the city council, themes such as energy transition, climate adaptation, nature-inclusive building and the circular economy are at the heart of spatial developments. I'M Binck – a platform set up by mobile project bureau OpTrek – has the ambition to give these themes a place in the area and bring them to the attention of local parties by building up a large network: consisting mainly of businesses still, but increasingly also the new residents (see Binckhorst Environmental Plan, Binckhorst Area Approach, Binckhorst Image-quality Plan).

Ambitions

Mobile project bureau OpTrek took the initiative in 2011 to settle in the Binckhorst with the mission to re-shape the desired area development by means of a bottom-up method and together with the users of the area. This method focuses on connecting to the physical, cultural and social structures of a place, and seeking collaboration with local residents, businesses, artists and designers to stimulate social, economic or cultural impulses. OpTrek's initiatives aim to pursue sustainable impacts by:

- Building connections that create more opportunities for local parties; vitalizing socio-cultural capital.
- Linking sustainability initiatives to boosting the local economy and creating cultural and societal added value.
- Giving the area's existing identity and history a prominent place in plans for the future.

In the early years, the independent area platform I'M Binck (Investeringsmaatschappij Binckhorst) initiated projects mainly together with businesses, but in the meantime initiatives have also been started together with present or future residents to make the Binckhorst a liveable, healthy and sustainable neighbourhood. Several rounds of interviews in which the wishes of residents were identified revealed that residents felt that the current character of the area but also the plans developed by the city council were rather 'dominated by hard surfaces'. Green spaces were lacking in both quantity and quality.

During an online meeting in May 2020, attended by people from the city council and the provincial authorities, developers, business owners and residents to reflect on the developments at the Binckhorst, the theme of 'green' was put on the agenda. There appeared to be great interest among all the parties to collectively think further about this topic and to flesh it out with tangible projects. The common goal was formulated as follows:

'Realizing a high-quality, green and climate-adaptive outdoor space. Where there is also room for recreation, enhancing biodiversity through small pocket parks, for example, and more opportunities for water storage.'[1]

One of the outcomes to emerge from these online sessions is the Bincks Groen partnership, in which the city council, province, developers and I'M Binck have joined forces to work together on greening the Binckhorst.

1 https://www.imbinck.nl/

'This is actually a very special group: everyone has their own interests, but the green theme has brought us all together. The desire to green the area was actually a kind of link between the different parties; in addition, everyone knows that greening the area cannot be achieved easily by individual parties alone.' (I'M Binck)

During the digital and physical working sessions, five working groups emerged, four of which focus on content for potentially promising projects relating to climate adaptation (temporary and edible green), green areas on existing roofs, running tracks in a green landscape and bee landscapes.

Collaboration and Process Method

Since 2014, the area platform I'M Binck has been organizing monthly networking events, which kicked off local momentum in the area's development. There are 10,000 people working at the Binckhorst but due to the spacious set-up of the business park and the individual nature of the activities, local businesses often did not know what each other's businesses did exactly. The networking events have changed that. Very soon, these contacts began to translate into physical connections as well; by exchanging goods (there are a large number of machines and tools to be found in the area, for example), but also by utilizing each other's knowledge, services and manpower.
In addition to networking events, I'M Binck has been initiating roundtable sessions since 2015. During these sessions, information on developments in the area is exchanged, but work is also carried out on a specific theme in a smaller group. Besides businesses, residents and other interested parties, officials from the City of The Hague and experts are at the table.

Many business owners in the Binckhorst are partners (financial or otherwise) of I'M Binck and participate in different ways in various initiatives (including sustainability initiatives). I'M Binck also collaborates with other organizations, such as Meer Bomen Nu (More Trees Now).[2]

A collaboration was also established with students of graphic design at the art academy in The Hague. The students explore how the development of the Binckplekken (see below) can lead to meaningful spots. There is also a collaboration with schoolchildren from Corbulo College in Voorburg. They are involved with Bincks Groen and learn how to make mobile planters from old pallets. This collaboration is one of the further developments of the theme 'Edible and temporary green'.

2   https://www.meerbomen.nu/

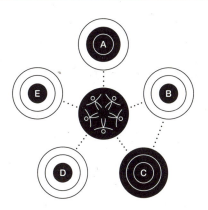

COLLABORATION

A   Designers
B   Government
C   Businesses
D   Ngo's
E   Education

I'M Binck　　　　57

Process Method:
'Leren kennen van mensen en plekken' (Getting to know people and places)

By organizing networking events, round-table sessions and expeditions, the I'M Binck platform connects local businesses, residents, the local council and other interested parties with each other and with the Binckhorst area. In this way, I'M Binck is pursuing the following goals:
'Making the qualities of the Binckhorst area visible and creating connections between users of the area and partners outside.'[3]

The monthly networking events give people the opportunity to get to know each other and keep abreast of each other's wishes, questions, knowledge, talents, services and products. This way, collaboration is encouraged.

The round-table sessions concern a particular theme related to the development of the area. All kinds of different parties – city council, professionals, local businesses and residents – can participate. Themes include facilities, mobility, safety or the green spaces. These sessions focus on the shared importance of core values specifically formulated for the Binckhorst.

By organizing expeditions through the area, I'M Binck makes the inherent qualities of the Binckhorst visible to interested parties. Showing people the area and discussing it gives people a different appreciation of a place.
'This was basically the city's dumping ground, where everything unwanted was shoved, and that has stuck in people's minds.' (I'M Binck)

These guided tours give people a different perspective on what the Binckhorst is now and what it could be.

[3] https://www.imbinck.nl/

I'M Binck networking event

Resource Cycles

Technical materials

Circularity was one of the focal points of OpTrek/I'M Binck between 2013 and 2017.
  'We started enthusiastically with this idea in 2013. At that time, the city council's reaction was something like "What on earth are you doing?"'
(I'M Binck)

One of I'M Binck's proposals was to establish a resources exchange in the area, in which I'M Binck itself would also play a role.
  'But something that has been a bit of a headache for us is that the city council itself hired a so-called resources broker. Externally. It was someone who didn't come from the area at all, didn't know the area, and so started from scratch again to take over all those contacts we already had. Unfortunately, nothing else of any substance emerged from this.'
(I'M Binck)

Nutrients

Besides climate adaptation, green initiatives at the Binckhorst also focus on increasing biodiversity and liveability: creating a pleasant environment for plants, animals and people. The ideas that emerged during the working sessions therefore relate to the resource cycles of materials, nutrients and water and focus on the following aspects: temporary and edible green, bee landscapes, natural purification of contaminated soil with fungi and bacteria, greening existing roofs and a green running and walking route through the area. From the vacant plots that will soon be built on, the initiators 'save' the young trees and shrubs that have sown themselves there and give them a new home on the 'CarWeide'. These and other cuttings and dug-up young trees can be collected here (tree hub) with the aim of drastically increasing the number of trees in The Hague, to slow down climate change and stimulate biodiversity. More than a thousand trees have now been planted on the CarWeide.

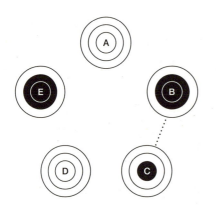

RESOURCE CYCLES

A Energy
B Nutrients
C Water
D Bio Materials
E Tech Materials

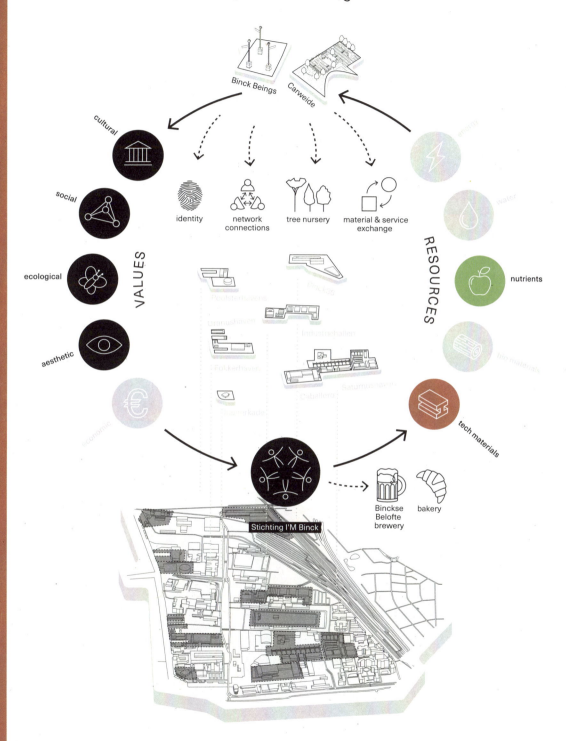

I'M Binck

Physical Developments

Binckplekken

In addition to the core values formulated by I'M Binck for the Binckhorst together with its partners, and which are now also described in the Area Approach and included in the environmental plan, 13 Binckplekken (Binck spots) – cultural and industrial heritage – have also been designated by the city council. These spots are scattered throughout the area as anchor points with the past. They are 'places of significance for the identity of Binckhorst due to their intrinsic cultural-historical value and a special programme designed to attract the public.' (Binckhorst Image-quality plan)

In the context of Bincks Groen, I'M Binck is now working on pleasant green pedestrian routes that will link the 13 Binckplekken together in a green walking network, so that not only the heritage spots themselves lend identity, but also the relationships between them. Creating multiple layers – history, visual-spatial content and programme – can generate added value.

CarWeide

In the middle of Binckhorst is the CarWeide, an empty plot designated as a traffic zone, and for that reason there are concrete slabs in the middle of the plot that function as parking spaces. I'M Binck has been given this plot on loan from the city council for five years. On the initiative of Bincks Groen, this place is now being activated, together with businesses and residents, to become a green meeting place and city stage. I'M Binck has already organized a number of talks here with The Hague politicians in order to embed the issue of greening better in the development of the Binckhorst. The location also acts as a plant and tree hub: in collaboration with Meer Bomen Nu (More Trees Now) [4], you can bring or pick up seedlings and cuttings here

Binck Beings, permanent markings in the public space

4   https://www.meerbomen.nu/

on certain days in winter. These were 'harvested' by volunteers locally or elsewhere in the country from places where they were in the way of people or construction work, and they are adopted and given a new home. In the zone surrounding the city stage, a temporary tiny forest is being created – a green oasis in the Binckhorst, which is dominated by hard surfaces. This place also acts as a stepping stone for insects, birds and other animal inhabitants of the city. The creation of green ribbons will connect these biodiverse spots with each other and with the Binckplekken, by means of nature-inclusive public space and façades. So a new temporary school is now being 'ecologically connected' to the CarWeide.

Binckhorst Beings

Eight companies from the Binckhorst have joined forces to exchange specific knowledge and skills. In 2016, this collaboration resulted in the Binckhorst Beings: 'permanent markings in public spaces that show what the industrial site has to offer.' With these works, the companies aim to strengthen the Binckhorst's identity as a makers' area.

Construction of the workshop space on the CarWeide

Stadslab session

Bincks Groen nesting boxes

64   Practical Examples

Values

The added value of I'M Binck's work lies first and foremost in bringing together and connecting people who have a link to the Binckhorst, and therefore in the social domain. In addition, the networks aim to share knowledge, skills and materials and, in so doing, develop connections that add economic value. A collective effort also makes a clear contribution to preserving and strengthening the Binckhorst's current identity in such a way that future developments can build on it.

The many initiatives relating to climate, green and circularity additionally focus on creating a sustainable area development that provides value not only on ecological terms, but also economically and culturally.

Once the first projects have been realized, Bincks Groen will contribute to ecological value, because the initiatives focus on increasing biodiversity and making the Binckhorst resilient to climate change by creating new green structures and spaces.

Bincks Groen also contributes to cultural value by creating awareness of biodiversity loss, heat stress and flooding, and by offering action perspectives to make yourself resilient to these aspects as a citizen or business.

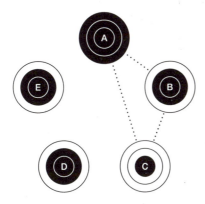

VALUES

A Social
B Ecological
C Aesthetic
D Cultural
E Economic

Conclusion

Network organization I'M Binck aims to contribute to the development of the Binckhorst into a sustainable and social district together with local businesses and residents. To achieve this, they have defined core values that every plan or development should satisfy. In addition, Binckplekken in the area have been designated to help strengthen the identity. Over the past year, greening the Binckhorst has been prioritized and I'M Binck is working with various parties to fulfil this ambition.

The interest and enthusiasm for I'M Binck's activities shown by local businesses – and also residents as they slowly arrive – is high, judging by the turnout at meetings and the submission of initiatives. The city council supported I'M Binck's networking events with an initial grant. Since 2018, these meetings have been co-sponsored by 'partners': local businesses or residents who contribute financially. Round tables are now mainly done as commissioned tasks.

'So if someone wants a round-table session, they have to pay for it. The income of our non-profit fluctuates considerably, which makes the organization vulnerable.' (I'M Binck)

And yet these connecting sessions are essential for the sustainability transition.

'A circular economy really leans very heavily on a community that is well connected in a very good way.' (I'M Binck)

The relationship with the city council has had its ups and downs. Although the council welcomes I'M Binck's initiatives, the high frequency of job changes at the municipal apparatus is not conducive to progress.

'At least five project managers have left in these last three years. And all the agreements we had made with one project manager in a year were no longer valid when the person left and disappeared without a trace.' (I'M Binck)

Without long-term commitment from the local council, which is responsible in particular for the area development of the Binckhorst, these kinds of loose partnerships are vulnerable and can also disintegrate quickly. Agreements on intentions, time and funds, with public and private parties, and other stakeholders, would enhance the permanence and sustainability of integral initiatives.

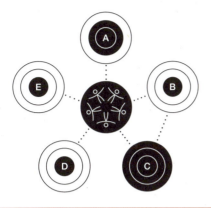

COLLABORATION

A Designers
B Government
C Businesses
D Ngo's
E Education

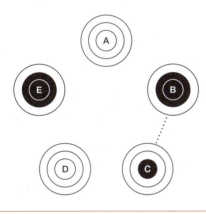

RESOURCE CYCLES

A Energy
B Nutrients
C Water
D Bio Materials
E Tech Materials

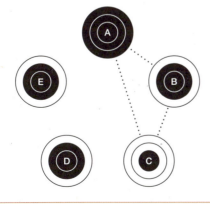

VALUES

A Social
B Ecological
C Aesthetic
D Cultural
E Economic

Schoonschip

 Buiksloterham, Amsterdam

Schoonschip is a floating residential neighbourhood in a side canal of the River IJ in the Buiksloterham area of Amsterdam North. The initiators' ambition was to develop the most sustainable neighbourhood achievable, with the boats being constructed as much as possible from sustainable materials, energy being generated locally and exchanged with neighbours via a smart grid, and water usage being handled in a smart way. After 10 years of making and implementing plans, 46 households comprising a total of over 100 residents are now living on the houseboats.

Schoonschip, the most sustainable floating residential neighbourhood in Europe

Ambitions

The initiators set up the Schoonschip foundation in 2011 with the aim of realizing a floating residential neighbourhood in Amsterdam where people could reside and live entirely sustainably. To achieve this, targets were set regarding energy and water management, but social ambitions were also high on the agenda. A tender document for the City of Amsterdam (2013) described these goals as follows:

- Affordable for households from diverse backgrounds across five income categories, including social renting
- An urban design that encourages a social living environment
- 100% renewable heating and hot-water supply
- 50-70% reduction in electricity requirements
- 100% renewable electricity
- 100% treatment of waste water and organic waste
- 100% own drinking-water supply
- 60-80% food production (fruits and vegetables) on own plot, using locally obtained nutrients
- Collective facilities such as shared cars, laundries, jetties and floating gardens.

These goals were then translated into an ambitious urban design plan, in which the various houseboats are connected by shared jetties. All the homes are connected to a smart grid so that energy is generated collectively and exchanged and settled up between themselves. The 46 households together have a single connection to the national energy grid. This way, Schoonschip becomes self-sufficient in renewable energy generation.

'A great many of the ambitions set out in the tender have actually been achieved, while some have been scaled back somewhat, for example concerning food production. But over the years, new goals and ideals have also been born and achieved, such as the collective space that has now been realized.' (VvE Schoonschip)

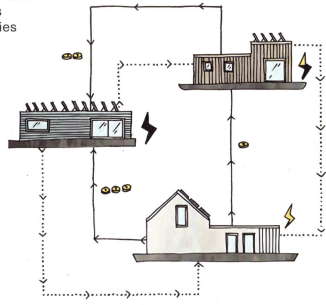

Via the smart grid, you supply your neighbours with renewable energy and you also consume energy they produce

Collaboration and Process Method

The Schoonschip foundation hired urban design firm Space&Matter to conduct a feasibility study into the Johan van Hasselt Canal site. At the same time, Metabolic conducted a sustainability study: how can the sustainable ambitions be translated into tangible interventions? What is financially and technically feasible? In collaboration with Spectral, a company specialized in developing platforms for energy exchange, Schoonschip explored how a smart-grid platform could support local energy generation, storage and exchange, in order to be as self-sufficient as possible through a local cooperative form of organization. By now, the organizational structure of a foundation has been replaced by an association of owners (VvE).

Together with Waternet, Schoonschip set up a pilot project to test a new waste-water system. This system separates grey and black waste streams, from which energy is recovered.

'This 'New Sanitation' pilot project was so new that it required a huge amount of consultation and coordination with Waternet, the City of Amsterdam, engineers and building-services companies. Not only from a technical point of view, but also organizationally, financially and legally, new ways had to be found. This was a time-consuming and costly process.' (VvE Schoonschip)

The relationship with the local council was constructive; the City of Amsterdam supported the initiative. During the time span of the process, which took 10 years from initiative to implementation, many officials changed position, which meant that certain matters had to be explained again and again. The innovative nature of the plans also clashed with the system:

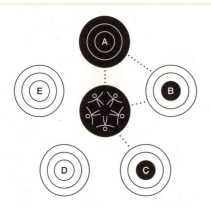

COLLABORATION

A   Designers
B   Government
C   Businesses
D   Ngo's
E   Education

'At one point, we got to a stage with the council where if someone called the contact person at the council, they responded with a sigh as if to say: 'What do you people want now?' It's as if you are making very complex demands all the time, but you also find that because of their system and rules, and the fact that we are doing all kinds of things that have never been done before, you still unintentionally get into very complicated processes. To which the council official has to say: 'Well, sorry, that's doesn't fall within our remit' (VvE Schoonschip)

Process Method:
Open Source Development

To make their sustainable floating neighbourhood a reality, the initiators hired design firm Space&Matter and circularity consultancy Metabolic to turn their dream into a functioning design. So there is a fairly traditional client-contractor relationship here, where the client is a group of private individuals and the brief is to design a residential area. The process of design and development is well documented and made available as open source, so that others who have similar dreams can learn directly from it.[1]

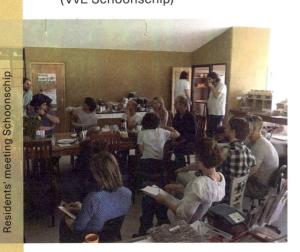

Residents' meeting Schoonschip

1   https://greenprint.schoonschipamsterdam.org

Floating gardens provide places for nesting ducks and swans

Resource Cycles

The ambition of the initiators of Schoonschip was to create a sustainable floating neighbourhood, while experimenting with closing resource cycles in various ways.

To maximize energy-neutral living, a number of technical solutions have been applied. For example, the houses are extremely well insulated, heat pumps are used to extract heat from the canal's surface water, solar panels have been installed and each houseboat has a battery to store excess solar energy, tap water is heated using solar boilers and heat pumps, and showers are equipped with heat recovery systems (WTW).

Water conservation and recycling solutions are also deployed to use water as carefully as possible. The houseboats are provided with a sedum roof that collects rainwater and there will be a separate flow for grey waste water and black water that will be discharged to a local fermenter, where biogas will be produced from it.

In addition, several Schoonschip residents share electric cars, scooters and bicycles and therefore do not have their own cars.[2] All knowledge gained during the development of Schoonschip is shared via an open-source platform, so that others can benefit from the lessons learned.[3] The community gardens, part of the initial ambitions, are still being built, but the ambition to largely provide for their own food production is proving difficult to achieve.

---

2   https://www.next-mobility.nl/oplossingen/huub-spot-en-app/
3   https://greenprint.spectral.energy

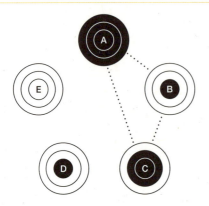

RESOURCE CYCLES

A   Energy
B   Nutrients
C   Water
D   Bio Materials
E   Tech Materials

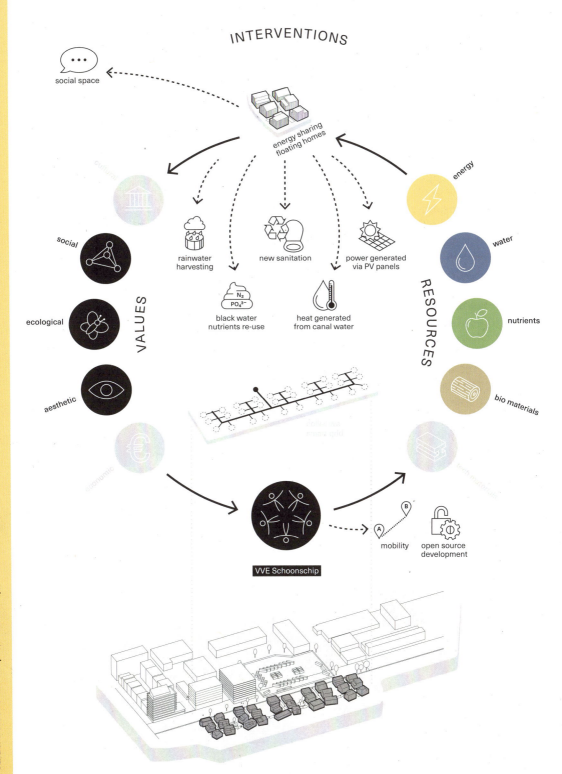

Schoonschip 75

Physical Developments

VvE Schoonschip owns the local energy infrastructure and delivers energy to the various households through smart control via a smart grid. With a grid like this, you can generate, exchange and settle up the cost of energy at a local level. Currently, it is not legally possible to collectively manage a shared energy supply and the current Energy Act specifies that an exemption must be applied for because the Act stipulates that energy can only be supplied by authorized parties. Schoonschip was able to get an exemption from the current Energy Act and shares on its website how to organize a smart grid like theirs.[4]

All the homes in the neighbourhood have sedum roofs, solar panels and solar boilers. In addition, the houses are constructed as much as possible from sustainable materials. A list of circular building materials was compiled and has been made available through the open-source platform. This materials list was advisory only; its use was not made obligatory.

Next to the bridge over the Johan van Hasselt Canal will be the location for Waternet's resources station, where the black waste flow from Schoonschip households, among others, will be fermented into biogas. However, this pilot has been delayed by complications arising from noise nuisance caused by the vacuum toilets and the provisional lack of a larger supply of waste flows from other homes or offices.

[4] https://greenprint.schoonschipamsterdam.org/impactgebieden/juridisch#net

Self-sufficient energy and water system

Schoonschip

Values

Schoonschip has a strong focus on the social value of the neighbourhood. The ambition was not only to form a close-knit community themselves but also to develop strong ties with the neighbourhood.

'It's certainly fine that you create your own little world with such a pioneering project, but how are you going to relate to the rest of the neighbourhood? Can we actually do something here that adds value for the neighbours in the Van der Pek neighbourhood? Or did we just make that up, and is this not really their thing?' (VvE Schoonschip)

The collective space for physical get-togethers has just been completed. It is a meeting space but other people and groups, for instance from the wider area, can also make use of it.

The added value of Schoonschip lies in the ecological sphere as well: experiments with local energy generation, new waste water treatment and sustainable building materials have led to a highly sustainable neighbourhood and a great deal of new knowledge being shared.

Spatial-visual value of the nature-inclusive collective space between the houseboats

In addition, the aim was to provide not only sustainable, but also affordable and social housing. According to the City of Amsterdam's tender, 30 plots were allowed to be developed, which would mean by definition that these would be pricey homes. In the tender, Schoonschip argued that 15 'decks' could be inhabited by two households, allowing cheaper housing to be realized. After resolving some legal wrangling, this approach succeeded. But the ambition of providing housing for lower incomes unfortunately proved unachievable.

'The price of the doubledeckers far exceeds the level of social rent. It also did not prove feasible to get housing associations to join further down the line.' (website Greenprint)

Besides ecological and social added value, the floating neighbourhood has, above all, aesthetic (or spatial-visual) value. The urban development plan allowed for great individual freedom in architectural interpretation.

'Within the frameworks of Collective Private Commissioning (CPO), there was still significant room for autonomy. You could choose your own architect and your own contractor. However, there is an urban development plan and a plot passport, and that has to be complied with. But if one of your neighbours goes in a direction that makes you wonder 'is that still allowed?', a lot of things are actually possible.' (VvE Schoonschip)

This has produced significant diversity in the homes.

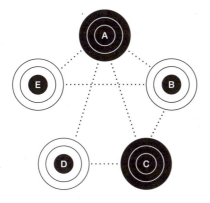

VALUES

A   Social
B   Ecological
C   Aesthetic
D   Cultural
E   Economic

Conclusion

By pioneering sustainable and social living on the water, Schoonschip has had to solve many technical, as well as legal, problems. As a result, there were years of delays, but in the end, the floating sustainable neighbourhood is there and the process is well documented so that it can function as a blueprint for others. The innovations followed on from the ambitions of the initiators who spearheaded this project and, despite the practical, legal and technical difficulties along the way, they have succeeded.

'Experts and professionals had not managed to achieve this result; they don't have the necessary perseverance. The local council should facilitate ambitions coming from the neighbourhood better. By giving the people who can and want this the opportunity to develop it.' (Space& Matter)

This does raise the question of how much time and energy you can ask from a resident in such complex innovation processes.

'It does sometimes border on "what can you do as an ordinary resident", in your spare time. It also involves a considerable amount of investigative work. And sometimes the authorities or agencies do not know the answer either. Then suddenly we are in the pilot phase, and they don't understand our question at all. That kind of pioneering problem.' (VvE Schoonschip)

Municipal bodies are also quick to offload responsibilities when things get too complicated.

'The interesting thing is, we have also learned, if you then cause a bit of a fuss, and you take it a step higher up, all kinds of things are suddenly possible again.' (VvE Schoonschip)

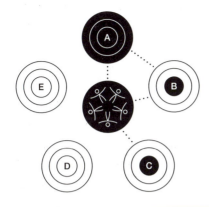

COLLABORATION

A Designers
B Government
C Businesses
D Ngo's
E Education

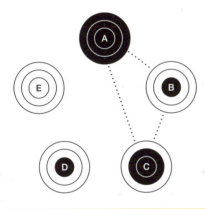

RESOURCE CYCLES

A Energy
B Nutrients
C Water
D Bio Materials
E Tech Materials

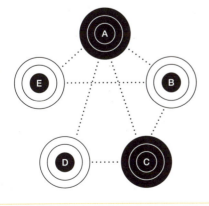

VALUES

A Social
B Ecological
C Aesthetic
D Cultural
E Economic

DeBlauweWij(k) Economie

Spijkerkwartier, Arnhem

The Spijkerkwartier, a neighbourhood traditionally designed for the well-to-do, fell into decline in the 1960s and 1970s. In 2006, the city council intervened, for instance by curbing prostitution. In 2007, the Spijkerkwartier was designated by the state as a protected cityscape. As a result of these measures, the Spijkerkwartier flourished again and is now a popular and diverse residential area. A number of citizens started a neighbourhood initiative for solar panels, Spijkerenergie, which subsequently grew into a network of numerous initiatives to realize an inclusive circular neighbourhood economy based on values already present in the neighbourhood. These initiatives have been brought together in deBlauweWij(k)Economie foundation.

Planting areas under trees in the Parkstraat with colourful, insect-friendly summer and winter greenery

Ambitions

In 2012, a group of Spijkerkwartier residents started the neighbourhood initiative Spijkerenergie, with the aim of collectively purchasing solar panels. After this collective approach led to successful collaboration with companies and the City of Arnhem and to results in the neighbourhood, this initiative grew into deBlauweWij(k)Economie foundation (dBWE). The foundation's ambition is to develop new business models based on local values that increase the ecological, social and economic sustainability of the neighbourhood. dBWE calls on local residents to contribute and realize their own ideas in collaboration with the local council, businesses and educational institutions, and by doing so, encourages local social entrepreneurship. By responding to local themes, it draws on the energy, knowledge and expertise present in the neighbourhood.

Besides Spijkerenergie, other initiatives have emerged, facilitated by dBWE, such as the BuurtGroenBedrijf in 2015 (greening the neighbourhood through climate-adaptive solutions), Spijkerbed (a collective neighbourhood hotel), Spijkerzwam in 2019 (growing oyster mushrooms on coffee grounds), the first two of which are now operating as independent entities. In addition, the BuurtBaanBureau connects work, talent and businesses in the neighbourhood and provides training for jobseekers, Spijkerbike reuses abandoned bicycles and the Circular Spijkerkwartier project works on reusing waste flows, for example by deploying worm hotels. dBWE operates from its own location in the neighbourhood, given the name DaZo (This Address Seeks Entrepreneurs). The most recent initiative is the BuurtKlusBedrijf (2022), which trains local people to become renovation specialists. By organizing implementation capacity locally, the energy transition can also become a realistic part of a neighbourhood-driven approach.

Collaboration and Process Method

For dBWE, an initiative for and by residents starts with a dream that one or more residents share. This dream preferably focuses on achieving a sustainable living environment. Next, the values this initiative could bring and which other parties could be involved are explored.

'We always look at the quadruple helix, so we always want companies, government and educational institutions at the table with us. We visit them and ask the question: 'This is our dream, what do you think of it?' And actually there is always an enthusiastic response.' (dBWE)

Interest cards are then completed by all the partners involved. This makes it clear what the intended added value is for the individual partners and therefore why they are at the table. From this beginning, a shared interest can then be formulated. It is crucial that this shared vision emerges from partnership:

'The current societal challenges we face are difficult to solve in a client-contractor relationship. You need to be at the table as equal partners to create the space to develop innovative interventions. This is a new process, for us as well, but we are a learning organization.' (dBWE)

DeBlauweWij(k)Economie works closely with the City of Arnhem's Living Environment team, with residents drawing up and prioritizing the annual development agenda and the resulting action list. Although the collaboration with the government runs relatively smoothly, the holistic and integral approach that initiatives inherently demand does not naturally align with this sectoral way of working in local government. Companies are more flexible in this respect and are quicker to see dBWE as a serious partner.

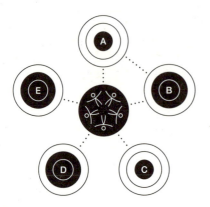

COLLABORATION

A Designers
B Government
C Businesses
D Ngo's
E Education

dBWE also works extensively with educational institutions in the so-called knowledge quarter. For instance, they supervise students from the Arnhem and Nijmegen University of Applied Sciences, and Wageningen University and Hall Larenstein University of Applied Sciences are involved in long-term research in the neighbourhood with Spijkerenergie, the BuurtKlusBedrijf and the BuurtGroenBedrijf. Erasmus University Rotterdam has recently started conducting research into what kind of value has been realized with the implementation of an initiative, and researchers also reflect on the collaboration between dBWE and the government.

Process Method: Shared Interests

DeBlauweWij(k)Economie's challenge is to connect the living world of residents with the system world of authorities. For this purpose, dBWE has developed a methodology – based on shared interests – in which the resident's dream or talent is central and forms the beginning of an initiative. Collaboration is then sought with local councils, companies and educational institutions that can help realize this dream. As equal partners, shared interests are identified, after which possible new business models are explored. This approach is based on three methodologies: Gunter Pauli's Blue Economy (2017), Jan Jonker's new business models (2014) and the ideas of the Shared Value Centre, a methodology that tries to provide insight into the values and interests of the various partners by means of a value map.

Process Method: Straatberaad (Street Council)

The BuurtGroenBedrijf has developed another method to involve residents in the redesign of their street: the Street Council. Here, too, the equality of the participants plays a central role.

The method has four steps:
- Contributing and Benefiting: how do you create a safe situation and how do you bring the level of knowledge to an equal level so that everyone can be an equal partner?
- Dialogue: everyone's interests come to the table where 'smart combining' is easier than making choices. Here, interests can be divided into 'own', 'shared' and 'general' interests, where the art is to combine own with shared or general interests. For example, the general interest of climate adaptation and own interest of having too many bicycles in front of the window could lead to the solution of a 'façade garden'.
- Draw up a joint Programme of Requirements, in which the level of ambition is defined based on six cornerstones. These cornerstones are: cultural history, spatial-visual features, management aspects, social aspects, climate adaptation and ecology.
- A jointly drawn-up Programme of Requirements is handed to a spatial designer.

Resource Cycles

Spijkerenergie aims to realize a CO_2-neutral and climate-adaptive neighbourhood. Here the focus is on saving energy as well as generating it themselves. For example, Spijkerenergie stimulates and mediates in the installation of solar panels, both as an individual installation on people's own roofs and collective installation on public or semi-public roofs (such as on De Lommerd community centre). Between 700 and 900 solar panels have now been installed through Spijkerenergie.

Spijkerenergie also devotes a lot of time and attention to informing residents, through information evenings but also so-called 'apple pie sessions'. In these sessions, Spijkerenergie engages with a small group of residents and provides insight into possible energy measures residents can take themselves. Using a roadmap, a diverse team from dBWE together with students works on a Neighbourhood Energy Transition Plan. In the plan, not only the technical side, but especially the social side is highlighted.

The BuurtGroenBedrijf (BGB) (2015) is a neighbourhood social enterprise that aims to:
  'create a green and social neighbourhood by taking ownership of the quality of our environment'. [1]

The BGB supports the construction and maintenance of communal indoor gardens, planted areas under trees and façade gardens, and organizes green cafés and neighbourhood safaris to share information and tips on greening and climate adaptation. The BGB is also involved in the redevelopment of streets in the Spijkerkwartier, after the sewers have been replaced. Through the 'Street Council', residents' wishes are identified, discussed and passed on to landscape architects as a Programme of Requirements. As part of the Circular Spijkerkwartier project, dBWE is now also engaged in cleaning up litter in public spaces. This is supported financially by a grant from the government's VANG (From Waste to Resource) programme.

[1] https://buurtgroenbedrijf.nl/

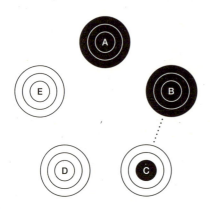

RESOURCE CYCLES

A Energy
B Nutrients
C Water
D Bio Materials
E Tech Materials

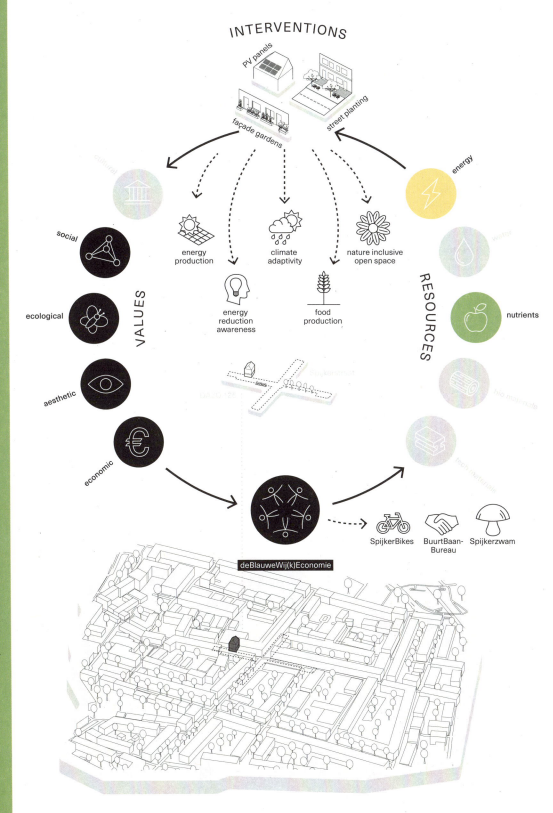

Recently, worm hotels have also been installed in collaboration with local residents. Spijkerbikes repairs donated bicycles that are then sold on or rented out. All these activities involve volunteers and provide meaningful work experience positions for jobseekers.

A group of residents has been engaged in producing oyster mushrooms on coffee grounds since 2019. The grounds are collected from offices by cargo bicycle, and are then processed into substrate for mushroom production. After a few mushroom harvests, the substrate is composted in a worm hotel. In this way, a residual flow is put to optimal use.

Local cultivation of oyster mushrooms on coffee grounds by Spijkerzwam

BuurtKlusBedrijf employees

Physical Developments

The physical impact of the circular initiatives of deBlauweWij(k)Economie and the BuurtGroenBedrijf are mainly visible in the Spijkerkwartier's public space. Through communal clean-ups, the neighbourhood is cleared of litter and greened by building façade gardens and addressing courtyard gardens. In particular, the construction of façade gardens and other plant and flower boxes and beds has given the public space in the Spijkerkwartier a completely different appearance. This is because the greenery is partly laid out and maintained by local residents themselves, resulting in a visibly different use of plant and flower species than the usual council planting. The changes in the public space therefore contribute to the attractiveness, liveability and uniqueness of the neighbourhood.

Green areas planted under trees and façade gardens

Values

The initiatives of deBlauweWij(k) Economie focus on creating a sustainable living environment in an integral and innovative way, where local residents work together with the local council, private companies and educational institutions. As soon as revenue models are viable, an initiative like this gets its own entity (see for instance the BuurtGroenBedrijf), but remains part of the dBWE family. The various initiatives have clearly realized added value in the area of ecology through the construction of indoor gardens and façade gardens, in sustainability by the installation of solar panels, and in the social and economic domain through the involvement of residents, especially those who are at a disadvantage on the labour market. dBWE has a strong focus on new workers, in particular to enable the energy transition on a local scale, by training people who do not have permanent jobs. They are given a smartphone application that allows them to watch introductory videos, after which they can put this acquired knowledge into practice under supervision.

After completing a number hours of work, workers are given a certificate for this skill.

'These local handymen and women are trained as renovation specialists and deployed to make homes more sustainable, but they also see what goes on behind the front door. We "collect" this social data as well, which gives us insight into both the state of the home and the well-being of local residents.' (dBWE)

Besides sustainability ambitions, the initiatives have in common that by creating awareness among residents, they are then more likely to become actively involved in a project and by extension in society.

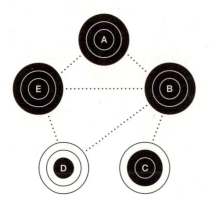

VALUES

A Social
B Ecological
C Aesthetic
D Cultural
E Economic

Greening the neighbourhood as a social activity that makes a positive contribution to climate adaptation and biodiversity

Conclusion

The collaboration needed to get civic initiatives like this off the ground does not always run smoothly. Firstly, the collaboration between residents: are there enough people who are willing to put time and energy into a project, potentially for a prolonged period? At Spijkerenergie, the initiators asked during an information evening who else would like to contribute to the initiative. Eight hands shot up. These eight people turned out to be willing to help with ideas on a monthly basis, but they were unwilling or unable to contribute more.

'That was when we began to differentiate between doers and thinkers. Because what we had were thinkers and not doers. It all worked out in the end and we created a kind of advisory group that included the thinkers.' (dBWE)

Although 15 per cent of residents are active in the neighbourhood and 35 per cent are 'awakening', half of them are still unaware.[2] It is very difficult to activate this group of people, because they often feel that you are representing an authority in which they have little trust.

Secondly, it is also often a matter of finding the right forms of collaboration between residents and agencies or authorities.

'We were confronted with the gap between systemic and living worlds, with the systemic world addressing societal challenges individually and sectorally. In my opinion, there is only one solution and that is collective. So, do we then work according to a sectoral approach, or instead integrally from how we see the living environment?

Integrally, of course. It means that that you have to do things collectively and integrally. This immediately makes it really difficult, but it is the only way to solve the issue. Therefore, that is the only way to go.' (dBWE)

Although design firms do not currently play a major role in dBWE's initiatives, there is design expertise present. The organization of the BuurtGroenBedrijf is in the hands of a resident who is also a landscape architect. Although she is a strong supporter of direct participation in design processes, for which the Street Council was also set up,

'it still always takes a designer to translate the expressed ideas and wishes into an integral plan'. (BGB)

The designers are therefore anchored in the neighbourhood's social networks here as well, which is why they can translate local needs directly into interventions, spatial or otherwise. The informal social networks of neighbours, friends and acquaintances and the formal social networks of local businesses create a social fabric in the neighbourhood, which is essential for the functioning of a society.

'When you have to resolve things with the government and commercial parties for yourself as an individual, it is often difficult. If you are supported by the social network in the neighbourhood, you see that a neighbourhood like this has a much greater support capacity. You have to keep nourishing the social fabric.' (dBWE)

---

2   https://www.lsabewoners.nl/een-bedrijf-maar-vooral-actieve-wijkbewoners/

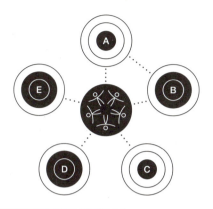

COLLABORATION

A Designers
B Government
C Businesses
D Ngo's
E Education

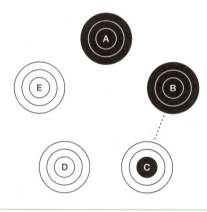

RESOURCE CYCLES

A Energy
B Nutrients
C Water
D Bio Materials
E Tech Materials

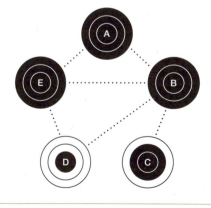

VALUES

A Social
B Ecological
C Aesthetic
D Cultural
E Economic

DeBlauweWij(k)Economie

Plant je Vlag - Iewan
De Vossenpels, Nijmegen

In Nijmegen, the city council made 200 building plots available for new forms of living and working. It called on ambitious citizens to plant their flag in the still-to-be-developed neighbourhood De Vossenpels, located on the outskirts of Nijmegen in the Waal river basin. Far-reaching participation in the planning, realization and management phases of the neighbourhood development was a key premise of this initiative, which was named Plant je Vlag.

Many homes in the now completed neighbourhood have been built with organic or natural building materials, such as wood, loam and straw. What is interesting about the development is that the visual quality (architectural use of materials, quality of public space) was not imposed from above, but was achieved through joint consultation at neighbourhood level.
In this case study, taking the example of Strowijk (IEWAN), a realized co-building project in De Vossenpels, we analyze the ambitions residents had regarding circular material use, how they went about it and what value was ultimately created for the neighbourhood.

The communal courtyard at IEWAN Plant je Vlag

Ambitions

Plant je Vlag was created as an experiment by the City of Nijmegen to gain practical experience with citizen participation as part of the new Environment and Planning Act. For the city council, the main ambition of the initiative was to democratize spatial development. This ambition was facilitated by the development plan drawn up (by consultancy firm We Love the City 2012), in which De Vossenpels was divided into several small communities, each with their own character and atmosphere. Residents were responsible for designing their own neighbourhoods. In this respect, a great deal of freedom was given by the council. There were no formal image quality requirements; local residents had to agree among themselves on the spatial conditions and ultimate appearance. The development plan put forward the idea of recording agreements per neighbourhood in a so-called image-management contract: a description of the shared ambition with regard to the character of the neighbourhood. In practice, this was not used by every neighbourhood.

Within the planning area of De Vossenpels, there were 24 existing houses covering almost 30 per cent of the planning area.

'The residents, some of whom are former market gardeners, value a green and diverse residential and living environment.' (Plant je Vlag, Vossenpels Development Plan)

The development plan used impressions to encourage organic development of the neighbourhood and the use of natural building materials by self-builders and co-builders. There were no further specific sustainability ambitions and requirements from the local council regarding the use of materials. This was left entirely up to the residents themselves.

Initiatiefgroep Ecologisch Wonen Arnhem Nijmegen (IEWAN) was the first co-building group to plant their flag in the area. They wanted to develop self-managed social housing and had high ambitions for sustainability, specifically in terms of material use. IEWAN drew up a detailed programme of requirements and budget itself and ultimately developed a customized ecological living environment together with architectural firm Orio. IEWAN describes the ambition as follows:

'Building and living sustainably and ecologically – that is a high priority for IEWAN residents. Building materials, energy concepts, building services and water management – everything takes into account production methods, consumption and CO_2 emissions. Fossil fuels are avoided. This has led to striking, innovative choices being made.' (Website IEWAN)[1]

[1] https://www.iewan.nl/

Collaboration and Process Method

'Plant je Vlag' is a 2011 initiative by the City of Nijmegen and Grond-exploitatiemaatschappij (GEM) Waalsprong. They asked the firm We Love the City, as spatial consultant, to develop a co-creation process and urban development plan for a sustainable Vossenpels with plenty of room for ambitious self-builders and co-builders.

During the initiation phase, We Love the City organized several meetings and on-site workshops on behalf of the city council, to which potential residents, businesses and other interested parties were invited and challenged to participate in the neighbourhood development. During these meetings, ideas were collected that were translated by We Love the City into a development vision (2011), which was then elaborated into the final development plan.

The development plan offered a great deal of freedom for residents' own interpretation, while clear frameworks provided clarity and certainty. IEWAN residential community's co-building project was created within this development plan.

As part of Plant je Vlag, IEWAN residential community developed what is currently the largest straw-construction building in the Netherlands. The complex, consisting of 34 social housing units (21 for self-contained and 13 for non-self-contained

Meergenerate wonen Nijmegen (MWN) and Initiatiegroep Ecologisch Wonen Nijmegen (IEWAN) realize their dream in Vossenpels

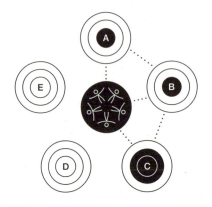

COLLABORATION

A Designers
B Government
C Businesses
D Ngo's
E Education

Practical Examples

occupancy), is built entirely of wood, straw and loam. That is why IEWAN is also called Strowijk (Straw neighbourhood). What is special about the development is that it involves social housing, with far-reaching collaboration at all stages of the project between the various parties involved. During implementation, for example, the relatively simple straw-construction method allowed residents, volunteers and professional construction workers to work side by side to realize the new residential building.

The idea for the IEWAN Residential Community originated at the kitchen table of the initiators, who at the time were living in a residential group at the Refter housing community in Ubbergen. Inspired by the stories of the pioneers at the Refter, they and some friends decided to create a new residential community of their own, 'this time in as ecological a way as possible'. The initiators of IEWAN wrote the plan and established contacts with the city council, housing association Woningbouwvereniging Nijmegen (WBVG) and Woningcorporatie Talis. After five years, they expanded the group to include fellow pioneers who also wanted to become fellow residents, if the plan succeeded. Talis was the financier of the plan and the City of Nijmegen and WBVG ensured that the project could be self-managed for minimal costs.

IEWAN engaged ORIO Architecten as the architect of the dreamed-of collective and ecological living environment. ORIO was selected based on their expertise in ecological architecture and straw construction in particular. Because of the special way of building with straw, the choice was made to develop the project in a construction team, which meant that the contractor was involved from the beginning of the process. Turnover requirements for the selection of the contractor were imposed by Talis housing association, the project's financier. Ultimately, contractor Vastbouw was chosen as the construction partner. They had no previous experience in straw construction, which at times created considerable challenges during construction.

Process Method:
Best Practice

To develop their Strowijk (Straw neighbourhood), IEWAN used the Best Practice methodology. The initiators spent a year visiting and analyzing a variety of ecological living environments at home and abroad. They ended up being most inspired by the straw-construction method, using wood, straw and loam, as applied in the Sieben Linden ecological housing project in Germany. By carefully studying this project, they were better prepared for the possible complications and difficulties they might encounter during the development and construction process. Ultimately, the method enabled them to work with the other stakeholders (housing associations, architect and builder) to develop a realistic and feasible proposal, in technical, financial and ecological terms.

Resource Cycles

Plant je Vlag is divided into several smaller communities, which are themselves responsible for the level of sustainability and image quality, with the minimum requirements of the Building Regulations naturally being met. With regard to closing resource cycles, it is interesting to look at initiatives organized at the neighbourhood level. IEWAN is a good model project because, compared to other projects in the neighbourhood, they had high sustainability requirements and a clear vision for the use of materials in their project.

IEWAN residential community based the design of the housing complex entirely on ecological principles. It is the only residential complex in the Netherlands of this size that was realized using the straw-construction method: straw bales are installed in a timber frame and then finished with loam. Besides the focus on ecological building materials, circular principles have also been applied at other levels to close the various resource cycles. For example, waste water is purified through a reed filter, washing machines run on rainwater and solar panels generate energy for their own use.

'Building with straw bales is an environmentally friendly way of building. Straw is a waste product. Many countries have a surplus of straw and in these countries, straw is burnt or worked into the soil. Growing and harvesting straw requires less energy than using other building materials. In addition, compared to trees for example, it has a short growth time (1 year). By building with straw, you produce no construction waste. Straw is a natural material and is biodegradable. Straw insulates against cold and noise. The heating costs of a straw-bale house are about 50 per cent lower than in a brick house.' (Website IEWAN)

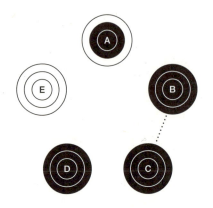

RESOURCE CYCLES

A Energy
B Nutrients
C Water
D Bio Materials
E Tech Materials

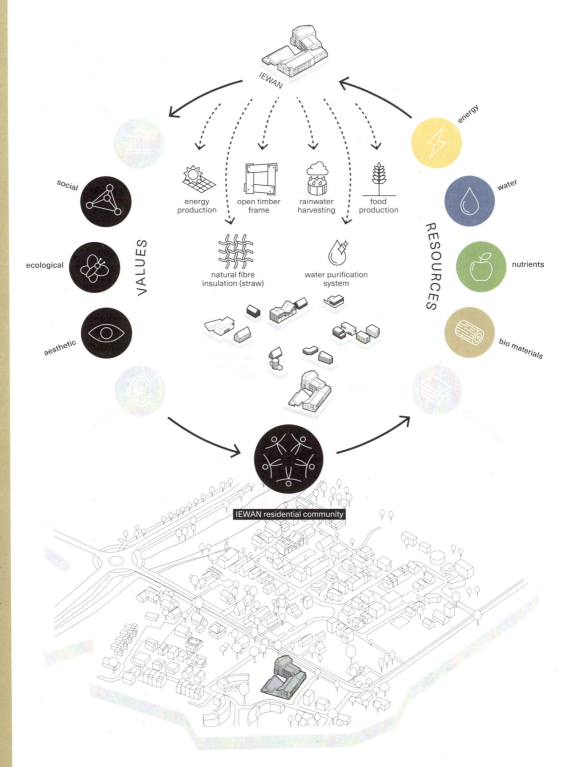

Physical Developments

It is clearly visible in Plant je Vlag that building without image quality standards results in a diverse neighbourhood. None of the houses or residential buildings developed on vacant plots look the same. Within Plant je Vlag, IEWAN forms its own community together with residential community the Eikpunt. IEWAN's development was derived as much as possible from ecological principles. The residential complex was built based on the following construction method:

'The future residents filled the timber frame with straw and finished the walls with clay plaster themselves. They were supported in this process by a total of more than 200 volunteers who gained experience in straw and loam construction while doing so.' (Website IEWAN)

The residential building is designed around a collective courtyard. This garden includes a helophyte filter with reed plants to filter waste water. The purified water is then used to flush toilets. Rainwater is collected via the roof of the residential building to provide water for washing machines. The green roof of the community building helps prevent surges on the sewer system, as the plants absorb the water, which then returns to the atmosphere through evaporation. A collective garden has been created around the building based on principles of permaculture, a sustainable agricultural method in which the land is cultivated following the example of natural ecosystems. This garden forms a stable ecosystem with a variety of plants that provide edible produce for residents.

Besides ecological principles, IEWAN is also based on the concept of communal living. These underlying principles are reflected in the physical development of the plan. For instance, residents share a laundry room, a communal living room and kitchen, several guest rooms, a bathroom with a bath, a work space with tools and a food cooperative (voko) for the collective purchase of organic food products.

'We want to live simply in a sustainable way', reads IEWAN's vision document. Residents were willing to sacrifice private space and live more compactly so that communal facilities and a green environment could be realized. The compactness of the design also has a positive impact on the sustainability and affordability of the project. Fewer building materials are needed and there is less space to be heated. With these underlying principles, IEWAN managed to keep the rents of the social housing in the plan low.

The residential community consists of 34 social-housing units, of which:

- 3 single-family homes
- 10 single-person homes
- 2 single-parent homes
- 6 two-person homes
- 3 residential groups
  (two with 4 people, one with 5 people – 13 units in total)

A number of workspaces have also been included in the project, which can be rented as offices, treatment rooms or studios. In addition, a multifunctional building, De Kleine Wiel, has been built in which residents can organize activities with each other, but which is also expressly intended for activities by and for residents of the whole neighbourhood (courses, performances, meetings).

De Kleine Wiel, multifunctional communal building

Plant je Vlag - IEWAN

Communal courtyard

Values

Within the Plant je Vlag development, there was plenty of room for experimentation by ambitious self-builders and co-builders. The development plan represented a minimal but clear framework that allowed organic development of the neighbourhood, plot by plot. IEWAN's example makes it clear that building on ecological principles can also generate social, aesthetic and economic value. Building with straw made it possible for residents to help build themselves, which ensured a high level of involvement right from the start of the development. The wooden cladding gives the building a sustainable character. The ecological aesthetic is further enhanced by the coherence between the residential building and the surrounding green outdoor space. Thinking in terms of closed cycles for water, energy and/or waste on a neighbourhood or residential building scale, and its visible incorporation into the collective domain, raises awareness about sustainability.

In economic terms, saving on water and energy bills ensures that housing costs can remain low, an important prerequisite for social housing. In addition, due to the use of natural materials and the compact design, the residential building performs better with regard to thermal insulation, saving even more energy costs in the long run.

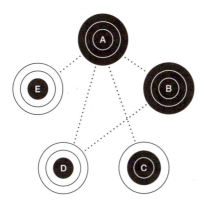

VALUES

A Social
B Ecological
C Aesthetic
D Cultural
E Economic

Conclusion

Within Plant je Vlag, the IEWAN model project shows that such an ambitious plan for ecological social housing is heavily dependent on the ambition and network of the initiators. The City of Nijmegen took on the role of facilitator and worked well with the initiators. The impetus provided by Plant je Vlag as an initiative supported by the local council created confidence among other key partners, such as Talis housing association and Woningbouwvereniging Gelderland (WBVG). In retrospect, a project like IEWAN might seem like a piece of cake, but interviews with the initiators revealed that a great deal of time was invested in achieving clarity in the plans and in convincing the various parties. For example, it took a total of three years to fully convince Talis housing association, the project's financier, of the feasibility of the plan. Before approaching ORIO Architects, IEWAN had itself already put together a detailed and financially calculated programme of requirements. In the end, in terms of design, the plan worked out exactly as the initiators of IEWAN had envisaged.

'During construction, it emerged that contractor Vastbouw's lack of experience with the straw construction method caused delays. For instance, Vastbouw did not agree with making the party floors of wood and suggested concrete floors instead. As a result, the supporting structure would also become less durable, as fewer straw bales could be used in the walls. IEWAN's design team stuck to the ideals and eventually the floors were implemented in wood, although with a cement screed. In this respect, model project Sieben Linden in Germany, which IEWAN had visited during the exploration phase, provided a great deal of sound guidance during the design and construction phase. The straw-construction principles applied by IEWAN in the project are almost identical to those of Sieben Linden. In hindsight, building with natural building materials has given Vastbouw many new insights; after completion of the project, a number of employees involved indicated that they would prefer to work only on organic building in the future.' (IEWAN)

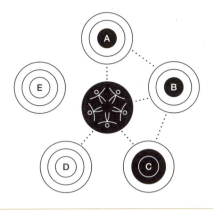

COLLABORATION

A Designers
B Government
C Businesses
D Ngo's
E Education

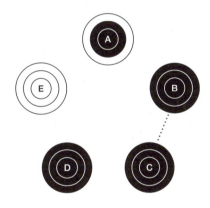

RESOURCE CYCLES

A Energy
B Nutrients
C Water
D Bio Materials
E Tech Materials

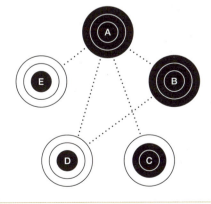

VALUES

A Social
B Ecological
C Aesthetic
D Cultural
E Economic

Delfshaven Coöperatie

Bospolder Tussendijken (BoTu), Rotterdam

The neighbourhoods of Bospolder and Tussendijken (BoTu) are part of the Rotterdam borough of Delfshaven and have a combined population of more than 14,000. For years, BoTu has scored poorly on indicators of safety, income level, well-being and health. The area is characterized by deprivation issues and the traditionally based efforts of the various municipal agencies appeared to have little ability to change this.

'Public investment resources are no longer sufficient and a closed top-down strategy is not the answer to the current problems.' (Veerkrachtig BoTu 2028)

Among other actions, residents have organized themselves in the Delfshaven Coöperatie, and together with public and private parties are exploring new ways of redeveloping, based on creating added value in and for the neighbourhood. Numerous sustainability initiatives have emerged from this cooperative. For instance, the neighbourhood installation bureau WijkEnergieWerkt and Delfshaven Energie Coöperatie started working on the theme of energy, with the main goals of achieving socio-economic resilience and accelerating the transition to an energy-neutral neighbourhood.

The playground at De Vlinder children's centre has been designed using natural and recycled materials, with a strong emphasis on nature inclusive planting

Ambitions

The Delfshaven Coöperatie was founded by residents in 2015 to operate as an initiator, facilitator and connector for long-term value development in the borough of Delfshaven. Together with a wide range of partners (including institutional partners), initiatives are set up and facilitated that encourage the local economy and community resilience. The Coöperatie does this by linking local initiatives to the ambitions of the institutional partners so that social returns can be achieved jointly (DHC 2015, 2017).

'Delfshaven has traditionally seen many residents' initiatives, and because citizens participate in multiple initiatives, a valuable ecosystem of local networks has been generated, on which cooperatives, local government and private companies can build further. And that makes it powerful and resilient.' (DHC)

The vision document 'Veerkrachtig (Resilient) BoTu 2028' describes a comprehensive programme in which many public agencies, private parties and citizens work together with the aim of making residents and the physical layout of BoTu economically and socially resilient (or more resilient) in the long term.

One of the developments the Delfshaven Coöperatie is working on is the energy transition for BoTu. BoTu has been designated by the local council as one of the first neighbourhoods in Rotterdam to be disconnected from the centralized natural gas network. The Delfshaven Coöperatie works together with the City of Rotterdam, Havensteder housing corporation and the IABR (International Architecture Biennale Rotterdam) to make sustainable energy accessible to everyone in BoTu, while at the same time using this transition to realize economic and societal added value. This includes ensuring lower energy bills for residents, community building and creating jobs in the neighbourhood. Neighbourhood installation company WijkEnergieWerkt is responding to this initiative. The aim of this company is to help people from the neighbourhood find work in the energy transition. Residents who have been out of work for some time, for example, are trained as solar panel installers.

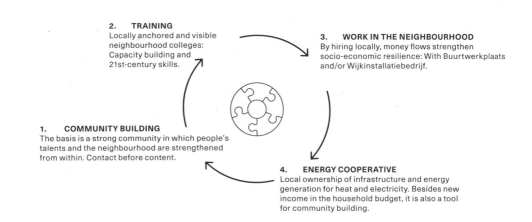

Energiewijk BoTu, making circular work of the energy transition

1. **COMMUNITY BUILDING**
The basis is a strong community in which people's talents and the neighbourhood are strengthened from within. Contact before content.

2. **TRAINING**
Locally anchored and visible neighbourhood colleges: Capacity building and 21st-century skills.

3. **WORK IN THE NEIGHBOURHOOD**
By hiring locally, money flows strengthen socio-economic resilience: With Buurtwerkplaats and/or Wijkinstallatiebedrijf.

4. **ENERGY COOPERATIVE**
Local ownership of infrastructure and energy generation for heat and electricity. Besides new income in the household budget, it is also a tool for community building.

Collaboration and Process Method

In 2016, on the initiative of the Stadsmarinier, a collaboration between the City of Rotterdam, Delfshaven Coöperatie, Havensteder and the IABR was created to achieve an integral approach in BoTu on the theme of safety. The 'Veerkrachtig BoTu 2028' programme is a follow-up to this but involves private parties in addition to these partners. For example, Rebel Group is engaged in implementing Social Impact by Design and energy supplier Eneco is a partner in the energy transition. In addition, a council of residents, the BoTu 12, has been appointed to advise on projects developed under the Veerkrachtig BoTu programme.

'The concept of socio-economic resilience underlying BoTu 2028 is great, of course, but what does it really mean for your actions? And now this council can advise on all kinds of development processes. A reality check of sorts.' (DHC)

The Veerkrachtig BoTu 2028 programme uses the '3x3 method': 3 themes (what?), 3 ways (how?) and 3 places (where?). (Veerkrachtig BoTu 2028, 2018) Besides the themes of 'healthcare, youth and parenting' and 'work, language and debt', the programme also includes the theme of 'energy, housing and outdoor space'. Within the latter theme, an integral approach is pursued in which energy transition and climate resilience are levers for improving both the liveability of the living environment and the socio-economic resilience of the residents. This integral approach is driven by three ways of working together: 'community building', 'social impact by design' and 'resilient professionals'.

The Delfshaven Energie Coöperatie, born out of Delfshaven Coöperatie's involvement in energy transition in the neighbourhood, and the neighbourhood installation company WijkEnergieWerkt are working with the local government, Havensteder and IABR with respect to the BoTu Energy District. In 2018, WijkEnergieWerkt received a subsidy from CityLab 010 to make this initiative possible. The company trains people to become installers to make homes more sustainable with floor insulation, for example, and to install solar panels. Participants receive training, work experience, a salary and a share of the profits. The neighbourhood installation company is part of a larger concept, working with Delfshaven Energie Coöperatie to install solar roofs on schools, in which local residents can invest as financing participants by purchasing solar bonds (200 euros each) or as supporters (25 euros). Profits realized partly flow back to the investors and supporters and partly into a neighbourhood fund, which is used to support residents with insulating their homes, for example.

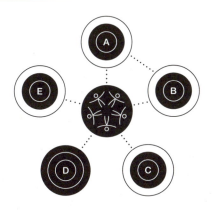

COLLABORATION

A   Designers
B   Government
C   Businesses
D   Ngo's
E   Education

Process method:
Social Impact by Design

Social Impact by Design (SIbD) is a method – based on Rebuilt by Design, which was designed for reconstruction work after Hurricane Sandy in the New York Metropolitan Area in 2012 – that seeks collaboration between the market, government and citizens who collectively search for new revenue models based on the urgencies and requirements of local residents.[1] The aim is to increase the adaptability and resilience of the neighbourhood and its residents.

'You can base this on numbers but also on existing networks and where the energy and needs are in the neighbourhood.' (Rebel)

SIbD is a four-phase process in which government, residents and private parties were invited to come up with ideas that contribute to BoTu's resilience. An open call was launched and widely distributed in Rotterdam, as well as nationally. The call received 50 responses, from which 28 entries were selected that were deemed promising for BoTu. Seven teams are currently working on implementing their submitted proposal.

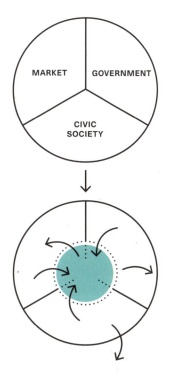

1   http://www.rebuildbydesign.org

Delfshaven Coöperatie

Resource Cycles

Energy

Delfshaven Energie Coöperatie is trying to organize the energy transition in such a way that money flows are kept within the neighbourhood and pay off there. For example, 910 solar panels are being installed on three schools. The roofs of these schools have been made available through a declaration of intent between the cooperative, the Rotterdam school umbrella organization Boor and the city council, and the panels are pre-financed by a maximum loan from the Realisatiefonds Energie Samen for 75 per cent, and 25 per cent by crowdfunding. Through this crowdfunding, neighbourhood residents can invest a small amount of money in renewable energy through the 'postcoderoos' scheme, which offers a 15-year exemption from energy tax on the solar or wind energy that participants collectively generate in a neighbourhood or district. In addition, the possibility is being explored as to whether energy can be stored in a smart way in neighbourhood batteries, allowing residents to trade in energy with their neighbours via a 'smart grid' and a smart meter. An experiment with 20 households is currently under way, in collaboration with the local council and Delfshaven Energie Coöperatie, which is exploring how self-supply through collectively obtained energy could be legally and practically regulated.

Through WijkEnergieWerkt, the neighbourhood installation company, people are trained to carry out the energy transition in the neighbourhood. After analyzing the possibilities in the neighbourhood, the initial focus of the neighbourhood installation company was on door-to-door sustainability, i.e., energy savings. By coming to people's homes, you can start the conversation about sustainability while already realizing some quick wins on the spot, so that people can see the added value for themselves.

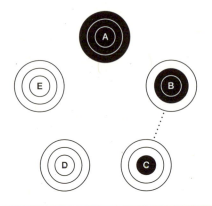

RESOURCE CYCLES

A Energy
B Nutrients
C Water
D Bio Materials
E Tech Materials

Practical Examples

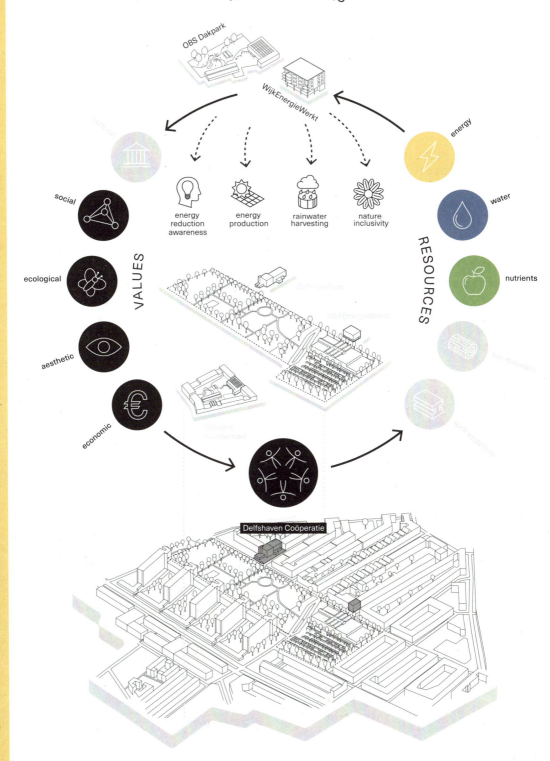

Value Flower Field Map Delfshaven Coöperatie

Delfshaven Coöperatie 117

'So we do simple things like installing reflective panels behind radiators, cleaning radiators, replacing lightbulbs with LED lights – basically everything people can do themselves in their home but often neglect to do. But where you can really save a lot of money. It will already save you about 150 euros a year on your energy bill, depending on the size of your house, of course.' (WijkEnergieWerkt)

Now that the solar roofs can be financed, workers are being trained via WijkEnergieWerkt and a professional company to install the solar panels. This professional company can then redeploy these people on future jobs.

Nutrients

At Dakpark primary school, not only will a solar roof be constructed in which neighbourhood residents can participate, but at the same time the outdoor playground will be planted with species that support biodiversity. A number of drainpipes have been disconnected from the sewer system and rainwater is chanelled into the schoolyard via an 'aqueduct'. In this way, children learn about sustainability in the neighbourhood in a playful way. The playground at the Vlinder school and the Driehoeksplein have also been redesigned with more attention for planting and a more friendly and natural playing environment.

By disconnecting drainpipes, the rainwater is led directly to the playground through these wooden construction

Local employees of WijkEnergieWerkt being trained

Physical Developments

Solar roofs

Solar roofs are being installed at three primary schools, Dakpark, De Boog and De Vierambacht, in which 180 residents have invested.

Zelfregiehuis

The Delfshaven Coöperatie has also been working on a plan to make the Zelfregiehuis (Self-Reliance House), where energy, healthcare, community building and economic development come together, more sustainable. The Zelfregiehuis is a place where people, especially vulnerable women, learn to take control of their own lives and work towards economic empowerment.

'Making the property ecologically sustainable can act as a leveraging tool to contribute to CO_2 reduction, but making a residents' initiative like this sustainable also ensures that places in the neighbourhood are taken out of speculative use, so that you build a kind of 'commons' of ownership of the neighbourhood, in the neighbourhood. Residents' initiatives benefit from continuity and slow growth.' (DHC)

However, while this research study was ongoing, the local council decided to accept the highest bid for this property and a dental practice will now be located here. The co-founder of the Zelfregiehuis has now found a new place in the 'Bollenpandje' together with people from the Veerkrachtige Gemeenschap foundation, to support local initiatives with her creative ideas. She wants to ...
   'green the neighbourhood and generate connection. We hand out plant cuttings and bulbs. The activities and programme in the Bollenpandje arise from questions and ideas from neighbourhood residents; the residents decide what is important.[2] The women who run this place have really made it very dynamic.' (DHC)

WijkEnegieWerkt employee on the solar roof being installed on Dalton school De Margriet

2   https://wijkcollectie.nl/project/botu0004/

Delfshaven Coöperatie

While redesigning the playground at the Dakpark primary school, considerable attention was paid to creating a natural playing experience

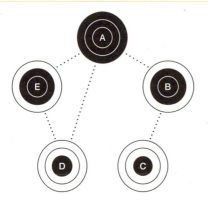

VALUES

A Social
B Ecological
C Aesthetic
D Cultural
E Economic

Practical Examples

Values

The added value of the Delfshaven Energie Coöperatie and WijkEnergieWerkt initiatives relating to energy transition lies primarily in the area of sustainability, as they envisage CO_2 reduction by cutting back heat and electricity requirements and switching to locally produced solar energy. Residents are also offered a low-threshold opportunity to become part of the energy transition themselves by co-investing in the solar roofs. In addition, the initiatives also contribute mainly economically by reducing energy costs and by creating local jobs through WijkEnergieWerkt. The company trains people to become solar-panel and insulation installers, and they can use this experience later to progress further in the labour market. Besides jobs, a local approach also generates social value by giving residents an affinity with the somewhat abstract concept of energy transition:

'Maybe the cousin of the people whose home we visit, who has been unemployed all this time, suddenly has a job in the energy transition through us. Then it becomes a positive thing and you really get a sustainable future. You are going to save money, you can find work in it, and your living comfort improves tremendously. Because in a lot of these houses we come to, there are draughts, or people can't get the house warm, or suffer a lot from damp. And we solve that for them.' (WijkEnergieWerkt)

Besides ecological, economic and social values, cultural value is also added by discovering new ways of working together with the market and government.

'This is an experiment in which we rediscover how we relate to each other. Working together at an early stage requires a certain vulnerability.' (Rebel)

'By involving people in the neighbourhood in developments and giving them the chance to be part of it and do it themselves, you simultaneously work on spreading knowledge and ownership in the neighbourhood, people's prospects for action and people's trust, and the stronger the network becomes. Through community building, local networks are getting stronger and stronger. The added value of local initiatives creates social, economic and cultural resilience that strengthens, enriches and embeds the plans of authorities in the neighbourhood.' (DHC)

Conclusion

The collaboration between local initiatives, such as those by the Delfshaven Coöperatie and Wijk-EnergieWerkt, is positive on the one hand and difficult on the other. The City of Rotterdam encourages these initiatives through subsidies such as Opzoomermee, the district commission's participation fund and CityLab 010, allowing them to grow and develop.

'So there is a healthy breeding ground for local initiatives, however only up to a certain ceiling: the point where it touches on the local council's framework contracts, tenders and concessions. Then the conversation gets tricky.' (DHC)

As long as the roles and working models fit within existing structures, collaboration goes well, but as soon as projects touch on different departments of institutional bodies, the conversation becomes difficult because the local council operates in a compartmentalized manner.

'That integral approach, it's just not there at all. And it is actually essential for this transition. In addition, the system often lacks a sense of urgency.' (Rebel)

The current playing field for neighbourhood development now often consists of public government authorities and private parties. This should really be expanded to a three-party playing field, and include much greater input from citizens or civic parties, which is what Social Impact by Design aims to do.

'It means that you get better and smarter plans.' (DHC)

The important question here is how to …

'… make an arrangement where you do justice to laws and regulations so that the risk of arbitrariness is covered, but also to the interests of individual residents or the collective, and where you give private parties space to do what they are good at.' (Rebel)

The full inclusion of citizens and civic parties in urban development also contributes to the continuity of process and project. In fact, this continuity seems to be guaranteed by the many local networks. Civil servants often change position:

'With the Urban Development department, I am already on to my fourth project manager in the area in five years. In essence, we are the memory for urban development. This is the schism between representative and participatory democracy. These are sometimes opposed to each other but they can actually complement each other well.' (DHC)

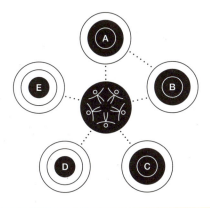

COLLABORATION

A Designers
B Government
C Businesses
D Ngo's
E Education

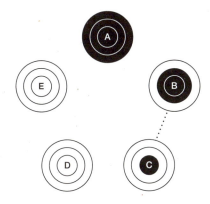

RESOURCE CYCLES

A Energy
B Nutrients
C Water
D Bio Materials
E Tech Materials

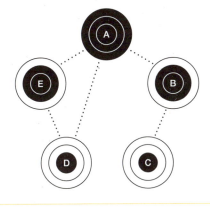

VALUES

A Social
B Ecological
C Aesthetic
D Cultural
E Economic

Delfshaven Coöperatie

Heliport Groen Initiatief

 Heliport, Rotterdam

Heliport (in de volksmond ook wel het 'kabouterdorp' genoemd, een verwijzing naar de puntdaken van de woningen) is een wooncomplex in de Agniesebuurt in Rotterdam Noord, gelegen tussen de Hofbogen en de Rotte. De naam Heliport refereert aan de landingsplaats voor helikopters die hier tussen 1953 en 1965 was en vanwaar vluchten naar Antwerpen en Brussel werden uitgevoerd. Na de opening van Vliegveld Zestienhoven (later Rotterdam – The Hague Airport) werd Heliport overbodig en lag het gebied lange tijd braak tot de vraag naar meer woningen in 1976 leidde tot het uitschrijven van een prijsvraag. De volgende voorwaarden werden hieraan gekoppeld: 'Eigen identiteit, individuele woningen, geen gemotoriseerd verkeer op het terrein, relatie met natuur op het binnenterrein én veel woningen op de begane grond.'[1]

Architect Jan Verhoeven won de prijsvraag met een ruitvormig stedenbouwkundig ontwerp waarin de woningen omgeven werden door een nieuw water, de Karnemelksehaven, afgetakt van de Rotte. Het plan voorzag in een verscheidenheid aan woningtypes, voor met name lagere inkomensgroepen, in een hoge dichtheid, gelegen rondom een centraal binnenterrein.

In 2017 leek dit binnenterrein volgens de huidige bewoners inmiddels meer op een parkeerterrein dan op een aangename plek om te vertoeven en daarom lanceerden zij een initiatief om van het binnenterrein een groene, klimaatadaptieve en fijne plek te maken.

Een door bewoners geïnitieerde nieuwe groene inrichting voor het binnenterrein

1 https://www.ookditisderotte.nl/blog/overig/kabouterdorp

Ambitions

At the Christmas drinks party in 2017, a number of residents had the idea that Heliport's inner courtyard was actually fairly dominated by paving. That is why the initiator and a number of other residents submitted a residents' initiative to the district committee to replace some of the paving with flowers and plants. The ambition was not only to develop a more pleasant inner courtyard, but also to be better prepared for climate change (both heavy rainfall and heat stress) and to stimulate urban biodiversity.

'It was a residents' initiative with a long-term vision: preferably greening the courtyard first and then perhaps the whole complex.' (Heliport Groen Initiatief)

With design agency Stichting Tussentuin, a plan was designed together with residents in a series of meetings in which 495 m² of paving was replaced with various types of plants and trees. Stichting Tussentuin had already been approached by the Rotterdam officials from the Water Sensitive programme, which focuses on rainwater in urban public space (among other things, aimed at relieving the pressure on sewers by disconnecting drainpipes), to investigate the practical feasibility of their programme.

The residents' initiative could also count on sympathy and interest from the City of Rotterdam and the Water Board.

'The city council noticed the energy and commitment of the residents: that's great, and suddenly there is a public garden here!' (Stichting Tussentuin)

They subsequently helped with thinking about and co-financing the realization of sewerage works and new, more sustainable playground equipment, in addition to the already-proposed greening of part of the site. Additionally, the drainpipes on the buildings surrounding the square have been disconnected and the rainwater flows through a marked point on the square to a reed-bed filter (helophyte filter) in the Karnemelksehaven. This way, rainwater does not go into the sewers and the influx of rainwater increases the circulation in the Karnemelksehaven, which improves the quality of the water.

Collaboration and Process Method

The Heliport initiators worked together with Stichting Tussentuin, the neighbourhood council, the City of Rotterdam and the Schieland and Krimpenerwaard Water Board to shape and implement their ideas for a green, social and climate-adaptive courtyard. Stichting Tussentuin, a landscape design and consultancy company, organized the discussions with residents and listed their wishes.

'An independent party like this does give more legitimacy to the project.' (Heliport Groen Initiatief)

The meetings for residents took place in a room on the courtyard itself, which they were able to rent at a reduced rate. Here, residents translated their ideas into mood boards. A separate participation process was followed with children and teenagers, during which their wishes (often wild) were identified using puzzles and games.

'This worked really well, because the organization level of the residents was so high; they organized the residents' meetings and we joined in with the design.' (Stichting Tussentuin)

The mood boards were translated into three concept plans by Stichting Tussentuin. Residents were invited to give their opinion on the concept plans via a Facebook group (600 members), a poster in the Helihonk (community space) and flyers from the city council. Residents could also vote online for their preferred design. Most votes went to the proposal based on organic forms.

The City of Rotterdam, the owner of the inner courtyard, became involved in the development and implementation of the design, including the simultaneous replacement of the sewers. The Water Board also saw opportunities in this development to improve both the water quality in the Karnemelkshaven and the climate adaptivity of the neighbourhood and it contributed knowledge, as well as financial resources.

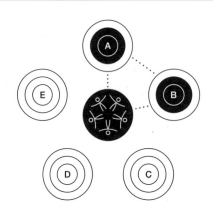

COLLABORATION

A   Designers
B   Government
C   Businesses
D   Ngo's
E   Education

Practical Examples

'It did take a long time before the City said 'Let's look at the planning schedules for when we can start tackling the sewerage system and bring things together.' In the end, however, they did. It took a great deal of effort, but finally the different schedules were brought together. It avoided the playground being tackled first, then the sewer and then the paving after that. Instead it meant putting all the work on one pile and tackling it right in one go. That is what happened here, and the City deserves praise for succeeding, despite the fact that it took a lot of time and energy to do it.' (Stichting Tussentuin)

The project was also made financially possible by Rotterdam Groen, a municipal action programme with the ambition of realizing 20 hectares of extra green space in the city in the period 2017-2021, together with residents, housing corporations, investors and businesses. The European subsidy programme LIFE, which focuses on nature, and environment and climate projects, also contributed to the financing of the greening of the Heliport courtyard.

'A number of projects in Rotterdam were selected for the LIFE project, including five in the Agniesebuurt, but two of these were not able to go ahead.' (Heliport Groen initiatief)

Heliport Groen was then proposed and approved as an alternative.

The City of Rotterdam is responsible for managing part of the courtyard, while residents take care of the other part. In practice, the residents and the council jointly take care of the entire courtyard. Residents feel involved and responsible for the area.

Process Method:
Residents' Initiative

A residents' initiative is an initiative by one or more citizens who want to improve the living environment in their neighbourhood or village. These initiatives can be aimed at improving the public space to make it greener, cleaner or safer, but also in the social domain: to improve the well-being of or social cohesion between citizens. Initiatives do need to serve a broader, more collective interest than just that of the individual. Local authorities have money available for financing residents' initiatives. Residents can submit their idea via a form and sometimes a verbal explanation.

At Heliport Groen, the idea initially arose among a number of residents to green a small section of the inner courtyard themselves. In order to develop this idea further and generate enthusiasm in other residents, a residents' initiative was submitted to the local authorities. This was approved and at the same time found so interesting by the authorities that it took on a larger role and worked with residents to green the entire courtyard and make it climate adaptive. The ambitions of local residents and the city council were in line with each other.

Resource Cycles

Nutrients

The initiatives of the residents of Heliport Groen were initially aimed at greening the inner courtyard by rearranging it with more trees and flowering plants that would benefit biodiversity.

'We wanted plenty of flowers for biodiversity, and also to attract insects and birds, so not just all those standard shrubs.' (Heliport Groen initiatief)

A 'worm hotel' has also been placed in the square, which turns biodegradable waste into compost that can be re-used for the plant and flower beds in the courtyard.

Water

There will be less pressure on the sewers, which have been replaced as part of the construction of the new square, as the drainpipes that normally lead rainwater to the sewers are being disconnected. At present, four drainpipes on the courtyard have been disconnected, and the others will follow at a later stage if the newly constructed system that leads the rainwater through an underground pipe system to a reed bed in the Karnemelksehaven works well. The influx of additional water into the Karnemelksehaven will hopefully also improve the water quality of the canal through increased flow.

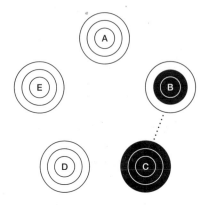

RESOURCE CYCLES

A   Energy
B   Nutrients
C   Water
D   Bio Materials
E   Tech Materials

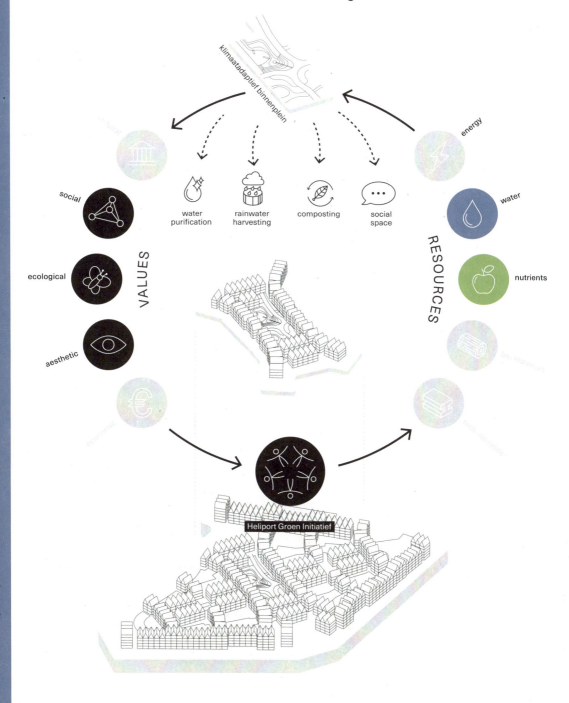

Physical Developments

Inner courtyard

In the sessions held to redesign the courtyard, residents preferred organic shapes for the plant beds and the path structure. Not only because this is more in tune with nature, but also because the organic shapes in the road make people drive more slowly. Apart from the slide, the new playground equipment is all made of wood.

Helihonk

The space adjoining the courtyard, which was first rented by Stichting Tussentuin during the consultation rounds for the design, has been taken over by active local residents who have renamed it Helihonk and use it as a social meeting space.

Water filter

The rainwater is channelled through gutters to the centre of the square, where it enters a well via stairs. At the Karnemelksehaven, rainwater enters the reeds, and after filtering it flows into the Karnemelksehaven and then into the River Rotte.

Disconnected drainpipes

Rainwater is filtered by the reed bed system

Rainwater from disconnected drainpipes flows to the well via 'stairs'

Values

The Heliport greening project has created added value for the neighbourhood in a number of ways. For example, disconnecting the drainpipes so that rainwater no longer flows into the sewers contributes to Heliport's climate adaptivity in the event of heavy rainfall, which improves water quality. In addition to added ecological value on the waterfront, ecological value has also been realized by increasing biodiversity. A selected variety of plants attracts certain insects and other animals. One year after the project's completion, residents already clearly notice the difference:

'There are a lot of extra insects and therefore birds in the courtyard, which were not there before.' (Heliport Groen Initiatief)

Working together to realize this initiative has created more social cohesion in the neighbourhood. The Helihonk meeting point and the agreement to maintain the planting beds together on the first Sunday of every month, named 'Groene Vingers', creates a sense of connection in the complex.

'Because you were gathering in the middle area, more and more people joined in. Now about 30 to 40 people meet up and help out.' (Heliport Groen initiatief)

Through shared responsibility for the square and its attractive character, the space fulfils an important social role:

'Before, residents hardly had any contact, but now we greet each other. The social fabric has become stronger.' (Heliport Groen initiatief)

Clear aesthetic added value has also been achieved by redesigning the inner courtyard; residents have been provided with an attractive and green space where they can linger, and it includes play facilities for children.

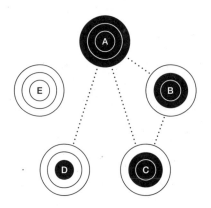

VALUES

A Social
B Ecological
C Aesthetic
D Cultural
E Economic

Helihonk as social meeting place

Planting of green beds was carried out with consideration for nature inclusiveness

Conclusion

Heliport Groen began as a residents' initiative with the ambition of greening the site by replacing a few paving stones with plants. But ultimately this was a first step towards a larger integrated approach, in which a number of city council departments were jointly involved in the planning and implementation. The fact that this was facilitated by a residents' initiative is not something that happens as a matter of course.

'There was a great deal of process involved: we had many discussions with different parties before we were taken seriously. We did have process funding to organize residents' meetings and to take the subject further, but it was a long time before the council said: let's look at the planning schedules for when we can start tackling the sewerage system and shift things to bring them together.' (Stichting Tussentuin)

That is why the integral approach and collective process was successful, in part due to the involvement of the city council. Thanks to the efforts of Heliport residents in collaboration with Stichting Tussentuin and the City of Rotterdam, the courtyard has changed from a paved car park to a green oasis. The changes not only make the area much more attractive, but also make it better able to withstand long, heavy rainfall and extreme heat.

'I think it has turned out to be a beautiful design with the variables that we had to work with. I am certainly proud of it.' (Stichting Tussentuin)

Stichting Tussentuin played a major role in the project, as designer but also as process manager, where they had to serve the interests of the initiating group, all the other residents and the city council. In the first phase of the project, the residents were the commissioning clients of Stichting Tussentuin,

'... because they approached us to make contact with the residents' initiative. In this situation, we worked together with them and needed the city council to make it happen. It subsequently became a project, where the city council was really our client and we had to serve not only the group of initiators but also the other residents, which makes you more of an intermediary. I think those two roles are also quite difficult to fulfil. At a certain point, this also gives you a different role in relation to the small group of residents you initially served.' (Stichting Tussentuin)

The social and professional network that the initiators already had, but greatly expanded through the process, was essential to the project's success.

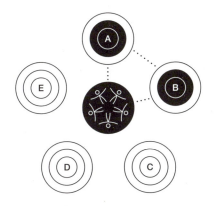

COLLABORATION

A Designers
B Government
C Businesses
D Ngo's
E Education

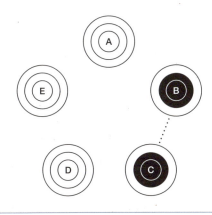

RESOURCE CYCLES

A Energy
B Nutrients
C Water
D Bio Materials
E Tech Materials

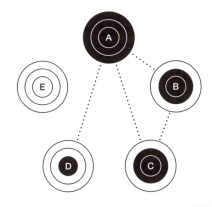

VALUES

A Social
B Ecological
C Aesthetic
D Cultural
E Economic

Insights Gained

The seven circular neighbourhood initiatives in this study were analyzed in a similar way, using the thematic layers from the Circular Value Flower. The various initiatives were juxtaposed to allow for comparison, with the aim of showing how these initiatives were translated into tangible projects and with whom they were developed, what the spatial interventions were and the values an initiative brought to the neighbourhood. The aim was therefore not to analyze the extent to which the initiatives differed or were similar, but mainly to learn from the divergent process methods for the benefit of future initiatives and initiators. The reflection and conclusions were considered on the basis of the following topics, using the Circular Value Flower analysis model, after which a number of recommendations were made:

- Towards a truly changed playing field
- Resource cycles, spatial interventions and value creation
- The circular value flower: from analysis method to process method

Towards a Truly Changed Playing Field

Collaboration

In all the neighbourhood initiatives discussed, the initiators – generally organized citizens – always seek collaboration with other parties, primarily with the local council, but also with businesses and other private parties such as design or consultancy firms and educational institutions. Collaboration with the local council in particular does not always seem to run smoothly in most initiatives. The council is a bureaucratic and rather cumbersome system with many different departments that are not always well informed about each other's project approaches and views. The holistic and integral approach that initiatives inherently demand does not naturally align with this sectoral way of working in local government. Initiators often appear to be faced with the gap between this compartmentalized system and their own perception of local processes. In addition, a large number of different people are often involved during the development process, which means the story has to be told over and over again to find support and backing. In the case of the Schoonschip project, for example, a new legal route had to be found to collectively generate energy and trade among themselves, because it proved legally impossible to do so under the existing framework. At both Afrikaanderwijk and the Binckhorst, the integral bottom-up approach did not match well with the sectorally organized local-government departments and money flows. The various neighbourhood initiatives show that collaborations are formed, but that obtaining equality between the various parties and realizing a level playing field as a result is not so easy, despite the fact that in most cases the various partners do have a positive attitude towards the initiative or project and want to play an active role in it. Often, a certain balance of power still remains, especially when there is a client-contractor relationship, as in the case of the Afrikaanderwijk Coöperatie's waste-recycling initiative. In the IEWAN project in Nijmegen, the collaboration progressed fairly easily, but here the city council had no direct interest in or influence on the project itself, only on the character and appearance of the Plant je Vlag overall concept. In Bospolder Tussendijken and Afrikaanderwijk, the initiatives had a direct impact on the local authorities' public tasks, which also meant that officials were more directly involved in the project. In the case of Heliport Groen, the ambitions of the initiators and the local government were aligned, so the collaboration went reasonably smoothly. The Stichting Tussentuin design agency also functioned as a 'mediator' between the city officials and residents. Stichting Tussentuin was able to 'translate' the residents' wishes into civil-service jargon.

Who Looks After Public Affairs and Interests?

The task of the government is to safeguard public interests, but the description of the cases strongly suggests that we need to adjust the perception that only the government can take care of collective values and that citizens only feel responsible for their own individual interest. On the contrary, we see active citizens involved in creating added value in the cases discussed. New forms of direct democracy, such as adopting a visual-direction plan with the neighbourhood (Plant je Vlag), will additionally anchor the legitimacy of other parties in the current (and dominant) representative democracy. Devising and implementing integral solutions to close resource cycles at the collective neighbourhood level therefore requires new partnerships in which the original tasks and responsibilities of the parties from the 'quadruple helix' shift. As yet, this does not seem to be a matter of course and is often complex, but by building on existing networks and tapping into local energy, circular neighbourhood initiatives can certainly lead to added value creation. Research has demonstrated that in these kinds of urban development processes, citizens often have to conform to local government decision-making procedures and legal frameworks for their project to succeed[1], even though these procedures and frameworks stop them from innovating. However, weak relationships between initiators and formal government institutions make scaling-up and innovation slower and more difficult. So both parties ultimately benefit from the forming of productive new partnerships.[2]

Potential Risks

The cases studied also teach us about the possible risks and pitfalls of such local initiatives. After all, these stand or fall with the contribution from active citizens who want something (have an idea or vision for change) and also have the ability (the energy, time and resources to be able to engage in it), on an often voluntary basis for a long period of time. DeBlauweWij(k)Economie, for example, noticed that despite the enthusiasm among neighbourhood residents about possible initiatives, the number of people who actually wanted to help organize them was actually quite small. They found a solution by making a distinction between doers and thinkers, allowing residents to indicate the way they want to contribute to a particular initiative. In addition, there are of course many residents who do not have the opportunity or simply do not feel like participating in neighbourhood initiatives as doers or thinkers. In any case, this group of people will have to be given the opportunity to have some form of say in another way, so that they too feel heard and there is sufficient support for the legitimacy of initiatives and projects.

---

1 Mattijsen et al. 2019
2 Franklin & Marsden 2015

Critics raise concerns that increasing influence of certain citizens on urban governance may actually increase inequality and segregation in the city.[3] As just indicated, the small group of active citizens who have the knowledge, resources and time to engage in an intensive collaborative process over a long period of time is often limited, and this hinders democratic, inclusive and broadly supported initiatives.[4] When few citizens develop collective initiatives in certain neighbourhoods (and this is then the dominant way that urban development takes place with no longer a centrally regulated programme), it leads to an increase in inequality and segregation in the social sphere – affluent versus disadvantaged neighbourhoods. The residents of Schoonschip, for example, are trying to connect with neighbourhood residents, but there are considerable socio-economic differences, which does not make integration easy. Collective initiatives appear most likely to succeed with a homogeneous group of people.[5] Differences between neighbourhoods also manifest themselves spatially, as Arnhem's Spijkerkwartier demonstrates. There, a group of residents made special efforts, successfully, to enhance the liveability of the neighbourhood by introducing planters, green borders and façade gardens. Neighbourhoods nearby, where these kinds of initiatives take place less often or not at all, now look very sparse in comparison. What is striking is that in both the Spijkerkwartier case and the Afrikaanderwijk case, the initiatives – created under the banner of deBlauweWij(k)Economie and the Afrikaanderwijk Coöperatie respectively – continue independently as soon as they can stand on their own feet financially and organizationally. A number of spin-offs have already emerged, such as the Wijkkeuken (Community Kitchen) in the Afrikaanderwijk neighbourhood and the BuurtGroenBedrijf and Spijkerzwam in the Spijkerkwartier. These 'incubator tactics' are generally associated with start-ups in the tech industry, but apparently also offer prospects at the local social level. At the Binckhorst and in Bospolder Tussendijken, these tactics would potentially also provide opportunities. Focusing only on the scale of the neighbourhood and on local initiatives can therefore lead to the disintegration of a city's cohesion into a patchwork of isolated neighbourhoods, causing the city as a whole to lose spatial and social quality – and therefore liveability. A clear framework (administrative and legal) within which neighbourhood initiatives can operate is therefore essential, while naturally always in connection with the lower scale levels (the street and the individual home) and higher levels (for instance, city and region). The analysis of the case studies paints the picture that by activating citizens, a facilitating role for government on the local scale and strong government direction on the larger scale (provincial, national, European, global), the transition to a circular economy can be broadly supported in societal terms and be successful. Greater involvement by citizens therefore requires support and some form of organization to sustain initiatives. A better balance between centrally organized government and individual citizens could be found in valuing and encouraging collectively organized local partnerships.

3 Fainstein 2010; Soja 2010
4 Durose et al. 2019; Uitermark 2015
5 Dietz et al. 2003

The Role of the Designer

In the projects analyzed, we see that the role of the spatial design professional is also changing in most cases. Domains for which the designer or specialist was traditionally responsible, such as the design of public space or the management of utility systems, are now (to some extent) also being claimed by empowered and knowledgeable citizens. In some initiatives, citizens also fulfil a role as designer and expert, for instance in Schoonschip and deBlauweWij(k)Economie, where the designer lives in the neighbourhood. In addition, the client is no longer automatically a government, private developer or individual; coalitions in which organized citizens have a large share in the commissioning process, alongside public and private parties, are becoming more common (see Heliport Groen). This means that the design process is organized in a less top-down way and moves more towards co-creation. As a result, the emphasis in a programme of requirements will shift and focus more explicitly on multiple value creation, with liveability playing an important role. The designer's role may also be more often at odds with residents' DIY intentions, because the residents' aesthetic and spatial perception may be different from that of the designer. In the Spijkerkwartier, residents greened the public space themselves, but were assisted by a landscape architect. At Heliport Groen, residents worked with a designer to redevelop their inner courtyard, after which the designer handled further arrangements with the various local government departments. In the IEWAN initiative, residents were very closely involved in the design and implementation of their communal housing project, but again they were supported by the expertise of an architect. The cases discussed demonstrate that the designer's tasks are being expanded and broadened. In addition to their design knowledge and expertise, they increasingly have a role as mediators between local bodies and citizens. In this context, knowledge of the formal plan and process stages, and skills as a process facilitator are essential. Additionally, the cases also demonstrate that designers need to have a high degree of knowledge of resource cycles in order to be able to integrate them into a plan at an early stage, to achieve multiple value creation in an optimal way. So, in addition to expertise on the ultimate form and appearance, process guidance and having an understanding of the technical and natural elements of ecosystems will have to feature prominently in the curricula of design courses.

Procesmethoden en activerend kapitaal

One of the selection criteria in choosing the cases was the use of innovative process methods for the design or development process. For each case study, this specific method is briefly explained in the section on collaboration. The method has deliberately not been evaluated but merely described; it serves in particular as inspiration for others. The methods described are all about shaping new relationships between or ways of working with the various parties as named in the Circular Value Flower. In some projects, these methods aim to balance the influence on the process between the various parties better and, in particular, give citizens a greater say (see, for example, Right to Challenge, Straatberaad, Shared Value Method). In other projects, we see that making existing or acquired knowledge transparent is seen as a clear added value to make relationships more equal (see Best Practice, Open Source, Knowledge Sharing). All the methods take as their starting point the importance of the participants' different insights and the importance of existing and future relationships. The cases show that citizens can take the initiative and responsibility for local processes in a wide variety of ways. The form of the collaboration therefore depends on the context and can take many different guises as a result. This situation requires considerable flexibility from the government to relate to citizens in different ways in various processes. To realize citizens' initiatives and enable multiple value creation, a coherent approach is essential.

Resource Cycles, Spatial Interventions and Value Creation

The circular neighbourhood initiatives demonstrate that there is plenty of experimentation at neighbourhood level with sustainable solutions to close resource cycles. Some initiators express an ambition from the start of the initiative to create added value by closing multiple cycles (see, for example, Schoonschip, IEWAN or Heliport Groen), while others start instead with a single cycle and shift their perspective to other resources if the first initiative is successful (see, for example, Afrikaandermarkt or deBlauweWij(k)Economie). Other initiatives take the existing parties and networks present in the neighbourhood as a basis for connection, which then results in ideas and projects for closing cycles (see BoTU and the Binckhorst). In all seven neighbourhood initiatives studied, we see that an initial idea starts from the energy, urgency and strength present in the neighbourhood and not necessarily from a problem, shortcomings and a predetermined process. The seven initiatives therefore start from a local perspective, demonstrating that sustainable added value can be realized on a variety of levels, not only in the area of ecology (which may be the initial focus of closing cycles for many) but also in social, economic, aesthetic and cultural terms. Multiple value creation was a conscious ambition in all cases and also formulated as such in the initiation phase. In this way, initiatives like these give substance to new value models for the neighbourhood, which are not only based on economic value, but where importance is also attached to other values, as is the case within the well-being economy discussed earlier. In all the case studies, people took the initiative with the ambition of increasing residents' well-being and liveability in their neighbourhood. Collective projects relating to energy and green (translated as 'nutrients' in the Circular Value Flower) appear to be favourites in this regard, perhaps because green projects take place in the public domain and energy projects can also bring short-term economic benefits at the individual level. In all cases, a strong link with spatial elements and consequently with the physical environment was clearly observable. The various initiatives show that realizing multiple value at the scale level of the specific neighbourhood or district in question has contributed to enhanced liveability (see, for example, the jobs created in Rotterdam's Afrikaanderwijk or the attractive and nature-inclusive public space in Arnhem's Spijkerkwartier or Heliport Rotterdam). A side note must be placed here as to whether the neighbourhood-specific initiatives are also replicable (usable in other neighbourhoods) or scalable (expandable in size or impact).[6] The initiatives analyzed are relatively small-scale and inward-looking, raising the question of whether closing resource cycles only at the local level will have sufficient impact to actually enable the entire transition to a sustainable society. The answer to that question is probably no, but that is not a bad thing. After all, closing cycles is facilitated by solutions at different spatial scales, from the level of an individual household, through the

---

6   Aiken 2017

neighbourhood, district and city to the region, the country and the world. It is precisely the combination of resource cycle solutions at different spatial levels connected to the various bodies involved in implementation that offers the synergy needed.

From Analysis Method to Design Method

The Circular Value Flower method, with the application of the visual Value Flower Field Maps at the basis, has proved itself to be a very useful and practical method of analysis. The initiator of deBlauweWij(k)Economie welcomed the Value Flower Field Map, as it shows at a glance the coherence of circular ambitions, spatial interventions and realized value. A visual overview like this would be particularly useful in communicating with officials, who are not always accustomed to thinking in terms of integral solutions.

A series of workshops, organized during our research with academic partners and NGOs in India (Bhopal), Kenya (Masaai Mara area), the Netherlands (Strandeiland) and Indonesia (Bandung), provided insights into the possibilities of also utilizing the Value Flower Field Map as a conversation starter to collectively identify shared circular ambitions and the paths towards them. The Circular Value Flower method proved to be a suitable design tool to make the complexity of the design process (from initiative to implementation and further development) manageable for initiators, layer by layer. It allowed them to shape an integral process themselves that led to local added value creation (for more information on these circular neighbourhood initiatives, see *www.circularcommunity.org*).

Lessons

From the research, we have distilled five recommendations addressed to local governments, citizen initiators and designers alike:

A Level Playing Field

In order to create a level playing field for circular initiatives, residents and businesses should be able to connect with the governance system in a low-threshold way, so that all participants have a real say and decision-making power. This increases citizens' prospects for action, giving more and larger-scale initiatives from a variety of initiators a chance to succeed. Currently, many circular initiatives get stuck within the local government's sectoral mill. Due to the integral nature of the projects, it is not always clear who is responsible from within the administrative system. Knowledge about circular neighbourhood development should be part of the proposed Omgevingswet (Environment and Planning Act) counter (one law, one counter) in order to support circular neighbourhood or district initiatives. A process facilitator operating from the local government (perhaps funded from neighbourhood budgets), with an eye for the integrality of circular neighbourhood initiatives and equality between the participants, could benefit the development process. The local-government system should also distinguish better between, and flesh out, the different roles it has in this regard: the directing and leading role and the facilitating role.

Focus on Existing Energy and Potential Synergies

Neighbourhood initiatives that focus on closing resource cycles fit well within the government's participation policy as a key pillar of the new Environment and Planning Act. In the early stages of initiatives, it is a good idea to look for networks and energy already present in a neighbourhood, which can be tapped into. The social fabric – the local networks present – in a neighbourhood is an important basis for collective circular initiatives. Local governments could share knowledge and skills gained from participatory best practices with new initiatives. In addition, multiple value creation can best be achieved if synergy is sought at the grassroots level between circular initiatives and other ambitions within a neighbourhood or district. This could also be managed at the local level, for instance through umbrella neighbourhood organizations.

Direction on Spatial Aspects and Liveability

Implementing circular solutions in the neighbourhood or district to close resource cycles has a significant spatial and aesthetic impact on the neighbourhood's appearance and local liveability. As local governments increasingly leave decisions about the appearance and programme of a neighbourhood (including the public space) to citizens themselves, the question arises of how to deal with divergent views and conflicting interests. Drawing up a visual quality plan for the neighbourhood or district with regard to circular solutions, consisting of a number of spatial and aesthetic principles (as is already done, for example, in a design control procedure), could give initiatives a clear (or clearer) framework for the desired development and potential opportunities.

The Role of the Designer

'Values-aware design' will increasingly gain importance This requires a different, more holistic design attitude from spatial designers involved in neighbourhood and/or district development (architects, landscape architects, urban designers etcetera). In that case, the power of design of spatial designers can be a valuable addition to a neighbourhood or community initiative. The spatial designer's ability to forge an overall narrative and depict the synergistic value that can be created by closing resource cycles can make it easier for different participants to achieve a shared vision. Visualizing circular solutions will therefore help increase support among various parties. Circular citizens' initiatives represent a new kind of task for spatial designers. Both citizens' collectives and the local government could consult designers as advisers, to help tackle circular community development in an integrated way. In the case studies, we have also seen that designers are increasingly taking on a developmental role and spearheading the set-up of circular neighbourhood initiatives, in consultation with organized citizens. The emphasis in a design on closing resource cycles additionally requires a great deal of new knowledge and expertise, which is also subject to rapid change due to new (technological and organizational) insights. In relation to this, the designer will have to adopt a flexible and open attitude.

The Circular Value Flower as a Useful Analysis and Design Method

As stated in the conclusions, the Circular Value Flower has proved itself as a useful and practical method of analysis when analyzing the seven cases in this research study. Additionally, as a process method, it provides a sound basis for identifying shared ambitions and ideas. This aspect of the Circular Value Flower method needs further investigation, and it would be interesting to also make the quantitative side of value creation by closing resource cycles transparent (measurable), in addition to the qualitative elements now presented. For instance, impact measurement by means of the Circular Value Flower could also be linked to the Sustainable Development Goals (drawn up by the United Nations), giving the method global and universal applicability.
The method can also be a good complement to the Participation Compass developed by the Dutch government in light of the new Environment and Planning Act, which serves to help citizens and local authorities develop participation processes.

Bibliography and Resources

References

Actieagenda Ruimtelijk Ontwerp 2017-2020: Samen Werken aan Ontwerpkracht. (Spatial Design Action Programme: Working on Design Power Together) https://samenwerkenaanontwerpkracht.nl

Aiken, G.T. (2017). The politics of community: Togetherness, transition and post-politics. *Environmental Planning* A. 49: 2383–2401

Arnstein, S. (1969). A Ladder of Citizen Participation. *Journal of the American Institute of Planners.* 35(4): 216-224

Bekkers, V., Tummers, L. (2018). Innovation in the public sector: Towards an open and collaborative approach. *International Review of Administrative Sciences*, 84(2), 209–213

Bosschaert, T. (2022), Circularity is not sustainability - how well-intentioned concepts distract us from our true goals, and how SiD can help navigate that challenge. In: *The impossibilities of the Circular Economy – Separating Aspirations from Reality.* New York: Routledge
See also: https://360dialogues.com/360portfolios/ce-impossibilities

Carayannis, E. G., Campbell, D. F. (2010). Triple Helix, Quadruple Helix and Quintuple Helix and how do knowledge, innovation and the environment relate to each other?: A proposed framework for a trans-disciplinary analysis of sustainable development and social ecology. *International Journal of Social Ecology and Sustainable Development (IJSESD).* 1(1): 41-69

Davoudi, S., Madanipour, A. (red.) (2015). *Reconsidering Localism.* New York: Routledge

De Bruin (2017) Participatiesamenleving anno 2017: volop kansen (Participation society in 2017: ample opportunities), Movisie.

Dietz, T., Ostrom, E., Stern, P. (2003). The Struggle to Govern the Commons. *Science.* 203: 1907- 1912)

Durose, C., Escobar, O., Gilchrist, A., Agger, A., Henderson, J., Van Hulst, M., Van Ostaijen, M. (2019). Socially smart cities: Making a difference in urban neighbourhoods http://smart-urban-intermediaries.com

Ellen MacArthur Foundation. (2012). Towards the circular economy: economic and business rationale for an accelerated transition. Ellen MacArthur Foundation.

Evans, J., Karvonen, A., Raven, R. (eds). 2016. *The Experimental City.* London: Routledge

Fainstein, S. (2010). *The Just City.* Cornell University Press

Florida, R. (2008). *Who's Your City? How the Creative Economy Is Making Where to Live the Most Important Decision of Your Life.* Basic Books

Fotino, F., Calabrese, M., Lettieri, M. (2018). Co-creating value in urban public policy contexts: A different approach. *Land Use Policy.* 79: 20-29

Franklin, A., Marsden, T. (2015). (Dis)connected communities and sustainable placemaking. *Local Environment* 20, 940–956

Gemeente Amsterdam (2020) Stadsmonitor Amsterdam (City Monitor Amsterdam).

Ghisellini, P., Cialani. C., Ulgiati. S. (2016). A review on circular economy: The expected transition to a balanced interplay of environmental and economic systems. *Journal of Cleaner Production.* 114(7): 11-32

Hajer, M. (2009). *Authoritative Governance: Policy Making in the Age of Mediatization.* Oxford University Press

Hajer, M. (2011). Signalenrapport 'De energieke samenleving. Op zoek naar sturingsfilosofie voor een schone economie' (Signal report 'The energetic society. In search of steering philosophy for a clean economy'). Netherlands Environmental Assessment Agency

Hughes, S., Hoffmann, M. (2020). Just urban transitions: Toward a research agenda. *Wiley Interdisciplinary Reviews: Climate Change*, 11(3).

Klijn, E-H., Koppenjan, J. (2015). *Governance Networks in the Public Sector.* Oxford: Routledge

Koefoed, O. (2019). Urban nature as transformed practice – A case of multi-dimensional processing to increase public value in Copenhagen. *Local Economy.* 34(6) 525–54

Kuitert, L. (2021) *The balancing act. How public construction clients safeguard public values in a changing construction industry.* Delft University of Technology

Lloyd, K., Fullagar, S., Reid, S., (2016). Where is the 'Social' in Constructions of 'Liveability'? Exploring Community, Social Interaction and Social Cohesion in Changing *Urban Environments, Urban Policy and Research.* 34:4, 343-355

Majoor, S., Smit, V. (2019). De wijk als plek van verandering (The neighbourhood as a place of change). In: Helleman, G., Majoor, S., Smit, V., Walraven, G. *Plekken van hoop en verandering. Samenwerkingsverbanden die lokaal het verschil maken (Places of hope and change. Partnerships that make the difference locally).* Utrecht: Academische Uitgeverij Eburon.

Mattijssen, T. J. M., Buijs, A. A. E., Elands, B. H. M., Arts, B. J. M., van Dam, R. I., & Donders, J. L. M. (2019). The Transformative Potential of Active Citizenship: Understanding Changes in Local Governance Practices. *Sustainability.* 11(20)

Meijer A.J. (2014). New Media and the Co-production of Safety: An Empirical Analysis of Dutch Practices. *The American Review of Public Administration.* 44(1): 17-34

Ministerie van Verkeer en Waterstaat (Ministry of Infrastructure and Water Management) (2016). Nederland Circulair in 2050 – Rijksbreed Programma Circulaire Economie (The Netherlands Circular in 2050 - Government-wide Circular Economy Programme).

OECD (2020), How's Life? 2020: Measuring Well-being, OECD Publishing, Paris, *https://doi.org/10.1787/9870c393-en*

Planbureau voor de Leefomgeving (Netherlands Environmental Assessment Agency) (2019). Scenario's voor stedelijke ontwikkeling, infrastructuur en mobiliteit – verdieping bij oefenen met de toekomst (Scenarios for urban development, infrastructure and mobility - greater depth when practising with the future).

Planbureau voor de Leefomgeving (Netherlands Environmental Assessment Agency) (2019). Circulaire Economie in Kaart (Circular Economy Explored). *www.pbl.nl/sites/default/downloads/pbl-circulaire-economie-in-kaart-3401*

Pomponi, F., Moncaster, A., (2017). Circular Economy for the Built Environment: A Research Framework. *Journal of Cleaner Production.* 143: 710-18.

Raworth, K. (2017) *Doughnut Economics. Seven Ways to Think Like a 21st Century Economist.* London: Penguin Random House

Reinhard, S., Verhagen, J., Wolters, W., Ruerd, R. (2017). Water-food-energy nexus: A quick scan. Wageningen, Wageningen Economic Research, Report 2017-096. *https://edepot.wur.nl/424551*

Rijksoverheid (Government of the Netherlands) (2019). Klimaatakkoord (Climate Agreement). *https://www.klimaatakkoord.nl*

Soeterbroek, F. (2015). Stadsmakers als happy infiltrators in de systeemwereld (City-makers as happy infiltrators in the systemic world). In: Franke, S., Niemans, J., Soeterbroek, F. Het Nieuwe Stadmaken - Van gedreven pioniere naar gelijk speelveld (The New City-making - From passionate pioneering to level playing field). TrancityXValiz.

Soja, E. (2010). *Seeking Spatial Justice.* University of Minnesota Press

Trebeck, K., en Williams, J. (2019). *The Economics of Arrival: Ideas for a grown-up economy.* Bristol: Policy Press

Uitermark, J. (2015). Longing for Wikitopia: The study and politics of self-organisation. *Urban Studies.* 52(13): 2301-2312

Van der Schot, J. (2016). Besturen met Burgerkracht, samenspel in de energieke samenleving (Governing with Citizen Power, interplay in the energetic society). Retrieved from: *https://www.duurzaamdoor.nl/sites/default/files/2019-02/Duurzaam%20Door%20Besturen%20door%20Burgerkracht%20proef5.pdf*

Van de Wijdeven, T. (2012). *Doe democratie - Over actief burgerschap in stadswijken (Do democracy - On active citizenship in urban neighbourhoods).* Delft: Uitgeverij Eburon

Van Dorst, M. (2012). Liveability. In: Van Bueren, E., Van Bohemen, H., Itard, L., Visscher, H. *Sustainable Urban Environments - An Eco-system Approach.* Dordrecht: Springer

Van Reybrouck, D. (2016). *Tegen Verkiezingen (Against Elections).* Uitgeverij De Bezige Bij b.v.

Wilcox, D., (1994). *The Guide to Effective Participation.* London: Partnership Books

Documentation Case Studies

Afrikaanderwijk Coöperatie,
Afrikaanderwijk, Rotterdam

Websites
- *https://www.socialevraagstukken.nl/right-to-challenge-in-rotterdam-meer-samenwerken-dan-uitdagen/*
- *http://wijkcooperatie.org/nl/profijt/right_to_challenge/*
- *http://open-overheid.nl/longreads/aanpak.html*
- *https://www.volkskrant.nl/nieuws-achtergrond/niet-de-gemeente-maar-een-groep-buurtbewoners-verzamelt-nu-afval-op-de-afrikaandermarkt-~bdf3250c/*
- Afrikaanderwijk Coöperatie: *http://wijkcooperatie.org*

I'M Binck,
De Binckhorst, Den Haag

Documents
- Gemeente Den Haag (2019). Plan Openbare Ruimte Binckhorst. *https://denhaag.raadsinformatie.nl/document/7832625/1/RIS303175_Bijlage*
- Gemeente Den Haag (2019) Beeldkwaliteitsplan Binckhorst. *https://denhaag.raadsinformatie.nl/document/7832703/1/RIS303199_Bijlage*
- I'm Binck (2017). Kernwaarden Binckhorst 2017-2030
- Superuse Studios (2016). Metabolische Analyse Binckhorst. *https://www.pulsup.nl/projecten/de_binckhorst/*

Websites
- *www.imbinck.nl*
- Stadslab I'M BINCK, Kernwaarden borgen in beleid en het gebied *https://imbinck.nl/wp-content/uploads/20190418-Verslag-stadslab9-COMPLEET.pdf*
- BinckPraktijkAcademie *https://imbinck.nl/speerpunt-praktijkacademie/*
- Binckhorst Beings *http://www.optrek.org/project/21/resourcecity*
- ReCourceCity de maakplek. *https://www.wam-architecten.nl/resourcecity/*

Schoonschip,
Buiksloterham, Amsterdam

Documents
- Tender document Schoonschip (2013)

Websites
- *https://schoonschipamsterdam.org/*
- Greenprint Open Source: *https://greenprint.schoonschipamsterdam.org/*
- Klimaatakkoord.nl: *https://www.klimaatakkoord.nl/serie-aanpakkers/aanpakker-schoonschip*
- Waternet: *https://www.waternet.nl/werkzaamheden/nieuwe-sanitatie/*

Plant je Vlag - IEWAN,
De Vossenpels, Nijmegen

Documents
- Plant je Vlag, Ontwikkelingsplan (mei 2012) – stedenbouwkundige Andries Geerse (We Love the City) in opdracht van GEM Waalsprong en i.s.m. de gemeente Nijmegen.
- Plant je Vlag - Kavelpaspoort (April 2014) – opgesteld door GEM Waalsprong i.s.m. de gemeente Nijmegen.
- IEWAN Huishoudelijk regelement (2015)

Websites
- Plant je Vlag: *http://www.plantjevlag.nl/plantjevlag/kaart-detail/woongemeenschap*
- We Love the City (stedenbouwkundigen) *https://www.welovethecity.eu/nl/portfolio/nijmegen-vossenpels*
- IEWAN: *https://www.iewan.nl*
- Omgevingswet: *https://aandeslagmetdeomgevingswet.nl/@163359/%27plant-vlag%27/*
- Werkgroepen: *http://werkgroepen.strowijknijmegen.nl/*
- Woningcorporatie Talis: *http://www.talis.nl/*
- Woningbouwvereniging Gelderland (WBVG): *http://www.wbvg.nl/*
- Gemeente Nijmegen: *https://www.nijmegen.nl/*
- Strobouw Nederland: *http://www.strobouw.nl/*

DeBlauweWijkEconomie (dBWE),
Spijkerkwartier, Arnhem

Documents
- Gulikers, H., Van der Sterren, H. (2019) Wijkontwikkeling van onderop (2): Een bedrijf, maar vooral actieve wijkbewoners. *https://www.lsabewoners.nl/een-bedrijf-maar-vooral-actieve-wijkbewoners/*
- Jonker, J. (2014). Nieuwe Business Modellen - samen werken aan waardecreatie. Academic Service
- Kramer, M. & Porter, M. (2011). Creating Shared Value – how to reinvent capitalism – and unleash a wave of innovation and growth. Harvard Business Review.
- Pauli, G. (2017). The Blue Economy 3.0- The marriage of science, innovation and entrepreneurship creates a new business model that transforms society. Xlibris

Websites
- *https://www.lsabewoners.nl/spijkerenergie-en-buurtgroenbedrijf/*
- *https://www.lsabewoners.nl/een-bedrijf-maar-vooral-actieve-wijkbewoners/*
- *https://www.lsabewoners.nl/samenwerking-met-de-gemeente/*
- *http://democraticchallenge.nl/experiment/de-blauwewijkeconomie/*
- *https://www.stad-en-groen.nl/article/28515/onderhoud-van-groen-houdt-niet-op-bij-het-tuinhekje*
- *https://www.wur.nl/nl/project/Impactmeting-BuurtGroenBedrijf-Spijkerkwartier-Arnhem.htm*
- *https://mijnspijkerkwartier.nl*
- *https://mijnspijkerkwartier.nl/groep/deblauwewijkeconomie*
- *https://www.han.nl/onderzoek/werkveld/projecten/spijkerkwartier/*
- circulair: *https://mijnspijkerkwartier.nl/uitgelicht/resultaten-ideeensessie-circulair-spijkerkwartier-17-december*
- *https://mijnspijkerkwartier.nl/pagina/deblauwewijkeconomie*
- *https://youtu.be/Ft7TPpt48HA*

Delfshaven Coöperatie,
Bospolder Tussendijken (BoTu), Rotterdam

Documents
- Gemeente Rotterdam (2018) Call for action Social Impact by Design
- Gemeente Rotterdam (2018) Veerkrachtig BoTu
- Impactmeting Delfshaven Coöperatie – rapport van de eerste resultaten. Erasmus Universiteit, Igalla, M., Edelenbos, J., Van Meerkerk, I. (2017).
- Delfshaven Coöperatie. (2017). Wat is Delfshaven Coöperatie?
- Delfshaven Coöperatie. (2015). Samenwerkingsovereenkomst Stakeholders Delfshaven Coöperatie
- Projectplan Zelfregiehuis – Open Oproep Designing a Community of Care

Websites
- *http://bospoldertussendijken.nl/*
- *http://bospoldertussendijken.nl/botu-in-de-media/*
- *https://www.gobotu.nl/*
- *https://www.gobotu.nl/governance-social-impact-by-design/*
- *https://www.resilientrotterdam.nl/initiatieven/veerkrachtig-bospolder-tussendijken*
- *https://delfshavencooperatie.nl/resilience/*
- *https://delfshavencooperatie.nl/energie-cooperatie-botu/*
- *https://overmorgen.nl/case/botu-als-next-generation-woonwijk-en-energiewijk/*
- *https://www.volkskrant.nl/nieuws-achtergrond/koning-willem-alexander-pleegt-onaangekondigd-bezoekje-aan-het-rotterdamse-bospolder-tussendijken-o-wat-leuk-het-was-hier-zo-n-griebeszooi~b1bc436f/*

Heliport Groen,
Rotterdam

Websites
- Rotterdam gaat voor Groen (2020) Groene meters maken *https://www.rotterdam.nl/wonen-leven/meer-groen-in-de-stad/*
- *https://duurzaam010.nl/nieuws/stenen-eruit-groen-erin-nieuwe-klimaat-adaptieve-binnenplein-voor-heliport/*
- AD (2020) Het 'Kabouterdorp' gaat op de schop. Wat gaat er gebeuren? *https://www.ad.nl/rotterdam/het-kabouterdorp-gaat-op-de-schop-wat-gaat-er-gebeuren~ac7d629c/*
- *https://www.ookditisderotte.nl/blog/overig/kabouterdorp*
- *https://rotterdamwoont.nl/items/view/107/Heliport*
- *https://indebuurt.nl/rotterdam/toen-in/heliport-pompenburg~104111/*
- *https://www.rvo.nl/subsidie-en-financieringswijzer/life*

Image Credits

Value Flower Field Maps and diagrams were created by or under the guidance of Mo Smit in collaboration with Koehorst in 't Veld.

Photos by Els Leclercq, unless otherwise stated.

Image position:
t = top
b = bottom

p. 22-23	I'M Binck
p. 38	Afrikaanderwijk Coöperatie
p. 43	Afrikaanderwijk Coöperatie
p. 46	Superuse Studios
p. 47 tb	Afrikaanderwijk Coöperatie
p. 52-53	Afrikaanderwijk Coöperatie
p. 54	Susanne van der Kleij
p. 56b	Marsel Loermans
p. 59	I'M Binck
p. 63	Marsel Loermans
p. 64bt	I'M Binck
p. 68-69	Susanne van der Kleij
p. 70	Isabel Nabuurs
p. 71	*https://greenprint.schoonschipamsterdam.org/impactgebieden/energie*
p. 73t	*https://greenprint.schoonschipamsterdam.org/impactgebieden/sociaal#werkwijze*
p. 73b	Isabel Nabuurs
p. 77	*https://greenprint.schoonschipamsterdam.org/impactgebieden/water#oplossingen*
p. 82-83	Isabel Nabuurs
p. 84	deBlauweWij(k)Economie
p. 85	Jan Selen - JAM Visual Thinking
p. 90tb	deBlauweWij(k)Economie
p. 93b	deBlauweWij(k)Economie
p. 96-97	deBlauweWij(k)Economie
p. 100	Ambitiebeeld uit het Ontwikkelingsplan van Plant je Vlag
p. 113	*http:/delfshavencooperatie.nl/energie-cooperatie-botu/*
p. 115	*https://www.gobotu.nl/veerkrachtig-botu*
p. 118b	Paul van der Blom
p. 119	Paul van der Blom

About the Authors

Els Leclercq

Els is an urban designer, researcher and lecturer at the Delft University of Technology and Erasmus University Rotterdam. She carries out research into new organizational structures for innovative urban processes and how these structures play a role in the transition to a sustainable built environment. She is also interested in how decentralized circular approaches can provide technical and societal solutions at a global and local scale. Here, active involvement of citizens, datafication and digitalization (or the 'smart city') and a just and sustainable city take a central position. Els holds a PhD from the TU Delft's Faculty of Architecture and the Built Environment. The title of her thesis was 'Privatisation of the Production of Public Space'.

Mo Smit

Mo Smit is an architect and works as a lecturer and researcher within the Chair of Architectural Engineering at the Delft University of Technology's Faculty of Architecture and the Built Environment. Together with colleagues and students, she studies and develops solutions for a circular built environment, where she focuses on the innovation of bio-based construction methods and processes. As a result of her activities in Indonesia, she developed a passion for regional architecture, self-build communities and bio-based materials. Recently she initiated Bouwtuin in the Netherlands: cooperative action research that focuses on the use of natural building materials from the region.

Credits

This publication was made possible by financial support from Leiden Delft Erasmus Centre for Sustainability, Programma Ontwerp en Overheid (Delft University of Technology, Eindhoven University of Technology, Wageningen University & Research) – part of the Spatial Design Action Programme 2017-2020, Ministry of Education, Culture and Science

Texts:	Els Leclercq, Mo Smit
Copy editing:	Leo Reijnen, Taal & Teken
Translation:	Christine Gardner, Schot in de Roos
Design:	Koehorst in 't Veld, Chris Boender, Benjamin Sporken
Lithography and printing:	die Keure, Bruges, Belgium
Papier:	cover, Cyclus Offset 250 gram page, Cyclus Offset 115 gram
Production:	Marja Jager, Maaike de Jongh, nai010 publishers, Rotterdam
Publisher:	Marcel Witvoet, nai010 publishers, Rotterdam

With thanks to: Annet van Otterloo, Diana Vergeer, Ellen van Bueren, Hanneke Beld, Jolanda van Looij, Josee van Linschoten, Lenny van Klink, Lizanne Dirkx, Machiel van Dorst, Mare Nynke Zijlstra, Marleen Buizer, Patrick Hoogenbosch, Robbert de Vrieze, Sabrina Lindemann, Sascha Glasl, Sophie Boot, Stefan Mol, Szymon Marciniak, Thijs Asselbergs, Yvonne van Sark.

© 2022 nai010 publishers, Rotterdam.

All rights reserved. No part of this publication may be reproduced, stored in a retrieval system, or transmitted in any form or by any means, electronic, mechanical, photocopying, recording or otherwise, without the prior written permission of the publisher.

For works of visual artists affiliated with a CISAC-organization the copyrights have been settled with Pictoright in Amsterdam.
© 2022, c/o Pictoright Amsterdam

Although every effort was made to find the copyright holders for the illustrations used, it has not been possible to trace them all. Interested parties are requested to contact nai010 publishers, Korte Hoogstraat 31, 3011 GK Rotterdam, the Netherlands.
info@nai010.com

nai010 publishers is an internationally orientated publisher specialized in developing, producing and distributing books in the fields of architecture, urbanism, art and design.
www.nai010.com

nai010 books are available internationally at selected bookstores and from the following distribution partners:

North, Central and South America - Artbook | D.A.P., New York, USA, dap@dapinc.com

Rest of the world - Idea Books, Amsterdam, the Netherlands, idea@ideabooks.nl

For general questions, please contact nai010 publishers directly at sales@nai010.com or visit our website www.nai010.com for further information.

Printed and bound in Bruges, Belgium

ISBN 978-94-6208-741-5
NUR 648

BISAC ARC018000, ARC009000

Circular Communities is also available in Dutch *(Waardevolle Wijken)*: ISBN 978-94-6208-739-2

and as e-book:
ISBN 978-94-6208-759-0